ordinary words

Si Philbrook

NeoPoiesisPress.com

NeoPoiesis Press, LLC

2775 Harbor Ave SW, Suite D, Seattle, WA 98126-2138
Inquiries: Info@NeoPoiesisPress.com
NeoPoiesisPress.com

Ordinary Words
ISBN 978-0-9903565-2-3 (pbk)

    1. Poetry. I. Philbrook, Si.

Library of Congress Control Number: 2015902748

First Edition

Printed in the United States of America.

For Alice and Josh
the real poetry of my life,

and for Anita

for everything.

manifesto

it is the poet,

it is the poet
who should reach out,
shout,
as loud as sudden death
with every breath
to the reader,

it is the poet
who should share,
dare
to reveal,
steel yourself
for honesty,

it is the poet
who should learn to speak
a reachable language,
a clarity
of thought,

it is the poet
who should give deference,
not hide behind
obscurity
and dusty reference,

it is the poet.

Contents

Fly Posters Will Be Prosecuted

A Georgia Moon at Midnight

Songlines

The Jackson Poems

The SoBo Sonnets

Joe Nobody

Jericho

Wind torn
dusky warm evenings
the sticky heat, oppressive

The old man, Jericho
sits whiskered,
holds a scuffed, dog-bitten stick,
I have listened to his stories
deep resonant tones
almost sung,

His rain fast laughter
river slow eyes
he smiles,

"We were wild then
we lived, burned
like prairie fires,
Have you seen a prairie fire?
Have you touched its sky-full flames?"

He holds my eyes
a moment,
head tips back and laughs
the wind

"Ha, boy
Live!"

Holds out his closed hand
to give me something
opens an empty palm,

Life is here
and gone,
live.

Eight Line Love Poem

Love is at times a gentle thought
I once forgot to say,
A flower I could not take
For fear I break its tender beauty,

Eyes I looked into for too long
And now am scared to see,
Eyes that looked right through my soul
And saw inside of me.

Down by the Canal

I met her in a smokey
old town bar
Down by the canal,
On a jazz playing
whiskey warmed night,
She wore a long red gypsy skirt
Held tight around her thin waist
White leather belt,
She smelt good, Sunday morning warm.

Drank cognac and read a book,
Kahlil Gibran,
I was intimidated,
Fascinated, intrigued,
Her beauty.

Her eyes
Lit by the flickering fire
Danced bright.

I was tongue tied
Tripped and tumbling,
Trembling, I said hello,
Hardly adequate.

We talked
She talked to me,
To me,
I bought drinks
Agreed too earnestly
Said too much,
She teased, laughed,
Held my arm
to see my wristwatch,
her touch,
She had to go
Meet a friend,
She said she'd see me
Maybe.

I walked home alone
down by the old canal,
The cold, stinking, dirty,
beautiful old canal,

Her touch.

Sitting on the Tube Thinking About My Girl

This is life
This dirty smoke-choked town,
Ugly paint-peeled tumble-down walls,
I love it,
I love the smells
Rough 'n' ready, giddy,
Intoxicating.

This is life
Rain soaked Saturday
Sodden streets,
Buskers playing out of doorways,
Saxophone sounds softer through the rain
City sharp days
Made rain soft.

This is life
Me and you
Kissing,
Soft-lipped, cold-nosed,
Tip-toe kisses,
Tip-toe touching,
Puddle jumping
Doorway to doorway.

This is life
Taxi cabs loud with diesel
The wind and rain
Umbrella blown days
Rain stained streets
Broken down old town tramps
Ask you for money.

My girl lives in the
tumble-down-town
Sounds of jazz,
Sounds of the haphazard
upside-down built city,
This is life
crackling firefly,
tinderbox life.

Scruffy

I went down to Covent Garden
To listen to the cappuccino machines.

I watched the scruffy lovers
playing beatnik tricks,
They wore tackety kickabout boots
Tied up with string.

She sang
as he tapped out a tune
on his tatty old acoustic,
It rained
It rained on their peaked black caps
and their odd socks,
They stole kisses from the rain.

I watched, I watched as
the touch-torn lovers
the lip-bitten lovers
the scruffy lovers,
kissed
touched
loved,

Tumble down days
Made tatty with love,

What we are
Is love.

Canal Song

I met him in a smoky
old town bar,
Down by the canal,

He made me laugh
I remember that,
He had such funny eyes,

We talked
I don't know what we said,
He blushed
I liked that,
The men I've known don't blush.

He interested me
That's all,
No big words, emotions,
He was interesting
Unusual, I suppose,

I left to see how Claire was
with the baby,
It was weeks before we met again,

Why couldn't he see,
Why can't they ever see
that love
can be slow.

Fragments of Love

We made love on her bedroom floor
to the sound of an old gas fire
and ticking clock
and our breath,
close,

It seems strange now
At home again
But time is nothing,
Age nothing,
All there is, all we will remember,
Is the gentleness of moment,

She held me
gently,
I loved her
And I learnt from her,
But I learnt only
that I do not understand love.

We listened to old jazz records
scratched and tattered
and more romantic for it,
And we lay in her bed
And she held me so tightly
as if I mattered
as if she needed me,
She told such lies.

I remember the panes of glass
of her attic window,
I remember I rubbed one clean
to see the snow on the tree ....tops
in the park,
And when I turned back
she was asleep,

I looked out again
Wintertime tumbling out of the sky

Sharp, crisp, cold,
Love is not like winter
but hurts
winter hurt.

Fragment of a Night

Drank Friday night
into Saturday morning,
Jazz bar juke box played Nina Simone,
Sweated out a chit-chat chat-up
With a bar stool floozy,
Ate peanuts,
I don't even like peanuts.

Torn

I want to hear a sound
that is not the wind,
Give me words that stay,
You touch
You gently touch,
Nose against nose
Kiss for kiss
Breath for breath
and you think that is love,

I want to feel a warmth
that is not the sun,
Feel you near me
With me in the cold
Hold me tightly
touch for touch
word for word,

I want a love from you
that is not torn by your desires,
Fire on burning fire is your love
I am burnt
And torn
And broken,
by your love,

I want to hear a sound
that is not the wind,
taking me
and leaving me torn.

Wood-smoking

Wood-smoking warm
Early autumn days,
The dampness of the leaves
And me,
Trying to light the fire
Giving up
and dousing it with petrol,
More than once I singed my hands.

That time I stuck the chainsaw in the tree
Me, and Dad,
He had to pull the tree down with the tractor,
We laughed,
There was such a crack
as it fell.

Wood-smoking warm
Early autumn days,
Lazily collecting the wood
Coughing as the wind turned,
Smoke choked eyes,
Sitting on the woodpile
Tea from the thermos,
All of this
These small things
Matter.

Laughing at the jokes
my father told,
The love,
The warmth of the fire against my face,
Sitting in the back of the tractor,
Bumping home,
This soft love
Is where I begin.

Wood-smoking warm
Early autumn days,
Quiet times spent with my father,

These gentle times
These small things,
Matter.

Sometimes

My Grandfather broke his back
for love,
He told me stories
Such beautiful stories,
I was the match-girl
became the Princess,
dances and chocolates
laughter and raindrops
All the words in all the world
were his.

My Grandfather died of cancer
I was too young to feel it,
to feel the loss
to understand the strength
with which he bore his pain.

Sometimes I think I hear his voice
his laughter,
Deep and unrestrained
Untamed,

His untamed love.

My Grandfather would have died for love
But he just died,
Is that how love is?
So unforgiving.

Joe Nobody

Joe Nobody lives down our street
I meet him almost every day
At the bus stop
Going shopping
Library books,

He looks at me
And thinks he sees
The girl next door
Quiet, shy, mousy hair,

I look at him
And think he thinks this,

We say hello
It's nice again,
He told a joke once
I didn't quite hear,
Embarrassed he repeated it
Embarrassed I laughed,

It would be easy
Just to say
    I like you
It would be.......easy
But we don't,

Is this how life is?
    Is meant to be?

Things left
    so quietly unsaid.

Friday Night

Friday night bites on her jaded thighs
Cigarettes and gin,
It's no sin to be lonely
Only don't come around here
Saying that you're sorry,
And don't come around here
Asking for money
She just don't fool so easy,
Friday night bites and its way too late
She's in a state, again
Late again, she can't afford another kid,
Cigarettes and alcohol
The bruises still show,
Last bastard bit her,
What a fuck.

Friday night bites and her kid's crying
Tried so hard,
Did the programmes
Did the time,
Bleeding liberal hearts ain't worth a dime
They're the ones who pay for it,

Friday night waits,
Everything slows with the cold,
Couple of cops told jokes and smoked,
Had to wait three hours to get the body taken,
Overtime rates.

A Bit About Buttercups

Close your eyes
Ha, cheat!

Read this then do as it says with your eyes closed.

Imagine
Imagine you are holding out your hand.
On the palm of your hand there is some earth,
  soft and fresh,
On the earth is some grass
still wet with dew,

Slowly
Up between the blades of grass grow a buttercup
Gently
With your other hand pick the buttercup, and place it in your heart.

Smile.

It doesn't solve all your problems
Or stop you being sad,
But it helps,
And next time someone asks you why you're smiling
You can tell them it's because you've got a buttercup in your heart.

Night

Do we love?
Have we ever truly loved?
Is it not enough that we must die
Without these lies
This tongue tied silence
Tear stained ignorance
Night
Broken by tears
Broken by dreams
Why are we here?
Why are we really here?

Ragamuffin

I am Christ on a hot summers' day sitting in a cornfield. If Christ were alive today he'd be working in a petrol station. That's a lie, but I work in a petrol station. Come meet humanity as it buys petrol. Humanity stinks.

I am Christ on a hot summer's day sitting in the cornfield. THE cornfield, definite article. It exists. Somewhere I've been to. Not the ones they tell you about in school. Listen boys and girls, there was a field-mouse who lived in a cornfield. Where is this cornfield? Alleged cornfield. The world is full of cornfields. Crap! The world is full of mars bar wrappers, coke cans, people who remember the war, and non-biodegradable plastics.

I am Christ on a hot summer's day sitting in the cornfield, smiling. If Christ had lived he would have smiled. He'd have been a bit odd though. The man you don't sit next to on trains. The drunk asking for money at Victoria Station. The prostitute outside King's Cross. Something seedy. Certainly something seedy.

I am Christ on a hot summer's day sitting in the cornfield. I have a nose bleed. Allergy to the new chemicals. Never mind you say. Borrow my handkerchief. Thank you. Brief, to the point, shows you care without giving away too much. We scratch the surface of each other so. What are we that we are alone so through the cold night? There were three American girls on the tube. Pretty. Hmm, yum yum. Talking about how the English didn't smile, didn't talk. That's me, what I am, an Englishman, definite article.

I am Christ on a hot summer's day sitting in the cornfield, yawning. Time is slow today, stretching in the sunshine. Life is slow. I stop, think. The smell of the kitchen when we lived above the café. The stairs to the attic room. Town noises. Headlight shadows across the bedroom wall. Aroma of coffee. So young. So very young, when time was young. An old man taught me chess sitting at the corner table. We lived in ..Brighton.. then. Mum and Dad ran the café. I learnt to swim at King Alfred's. Had a pair of roller skates. School was big and I was no good at football. We lived in ..Brighton.. and I grew up, scruffily.

I am Christ on a hot summer's day sitting in the cornfield. My nose is still bleeding. Paula had a nose bleed the day we went to ....London..... Italian students. They bought English music and postcards of the Queen. Antonio had his hair dyed green. There was trouble for that. I was student leader, joe responsible. I'd lied about my age. Twenty sounded so much older that nineteen. So there I was, Teacher of English with additional responsibility for hair colour. It was a good summer with the Italians. Gentle flirting with Paula. A brush past, a touch too long. She kissed me once. The last day as they left. Just reached up and kissed me. Unprepared I smiled. Gentle things.

I am Christ on a hot summer's day sitting in the cornfield, and I am bored. I do not feel. I scratch myself with a corn stick, just to know I am still there. I do not care and I do not feel. What are you? Helen asked me. Young girls are armed with pertinent questions, by their mothers I think. What am I? Am, such a definite word, so this or that.

I am a teller of lies, a player of games, a ragamuffin. Holder of dreams, keeper of secrets, ragamuffin. I like the word. It smells of me. What have I done? I have done whatever I choose to have done. There were four boys in the playground. They ran a race. Lee and Simon and Matthew and Michael. Lee was fastest, but this time, oh yes this time I was winning. He fell over. Mat and Michael kept running. I stopped. The attendant said I tripped him. I did not. Stand by the wall and do not move for the rest of lunchtime. I WILL NOT. Do as you're told. I DID NOT TRIP HIM. I saw you do it. I DID NOT. I didn't understand. I didn't do it. It wasn't me. How often had I told that lie. But not this time. This time she tumble tripped me with her words. Her grown up big world words. I believed. Everything was bigger than my eyes could see, my ears could hear, my nose could sniffle. Everything was big and I was sorry. I didn't mean to trip him.

Rag-tag-rag-a-muffin. Games I have played. Lies I have told. I think, when you have lied about love, you have told every lie. I love you is not a game to cheat at. (I have told every lie). There was cat in the road, run over. Crushed utterly. Half decayed it smelt bad, like us, we smell bad, in our shopping centres, restaurants, petrol stations. We stink. Love is that way when you tell every lie. You are the stinking cat in the road, fly-ridden, kissing with maggot breath as you pant and gasp your lies out.

The cornfield is a hot place. Sweaty. The grass round the edge still long, green, fresh, verdant even, but the corn is so dry, scratchy and buzzy with flies. Cornfields are not what they're made out to be. The pastoral, postcard world is dead. We sprayed it to death. It coughed, choked, spluttered, died. Who cares anyway? The world is not a real place. It can't be touched, just watched on television. Nothing is real unless it smacks us in the teeth.

The trick for sitting in cornfields, and there's always a trick (a wooden horse, a landmine, an encouraging smile) the trick is to look up. Be constantly aware of the sky. It gives a sense of the size of things. We look too much to the ground, scratching and crawling around on it. Our field of vision confines our lives, limits us. It makes us stronger when we are not afraid of the sky. I sit in the cornfield. Old shorts, cotton shirt. My legs are scratched. Red-touched from the dryness of the corn. There is a stream in the corner. Shoes disappear in a kick of the wind. Paddlesplashing. It's colder than it looks. What else is cold kiddies? Ice-cream, yes that's right. And? An Eskimo's nose. The east wind. An empty bed. Silence.

Rag-tag-tag-a-muffin. It's like Roge-dodge-dolphin. I met him. We went bowling. No really. He was in the next lane of course. With his girlfriend, Kate. I've known three Kates, but this was the best one. A fine woman of a Kate. The first was bubbly and fun. The second aloof, an art student, but this one, oh she was special. She was Kate, his girlfriend, but she could have been anyone, anything she wanted, a rare gift. I, of course behaved badly. Somewhere else, some other time we'd have got on, been friends. If we'd met in a bazaar in ....Cairo...., or a library, or on a long train journey, or as children in the café. I could have taught her chess. I hope she turns out to be a sculptor, or a poet or something.

It is strange what we become. This generation. We did not fight the War. We did not march with the peace movement. What is there for us to be heroic about? Angry about? We have watched too many war films. It has all been done. We are empty, directionless. There are no more Bogarts, just football thugs. We can't be heroes so we end up as spinning tops. Roge-dodge-dolphin, Rag-tag-tag-a-muffin. It's the same, tumble turning in our giddy, dizzy wind spun lives. We, the young don't care. We spit, and even as we spit we feel nothing. We are indifferent. Perhaps this should be more personal. I am all these things. I'm sitting here in this fucking cornfield getting sunburn, because I don't care. That's why Kate's important. She cares. It attracts me. Moths get burned. Perhaps I am just stupid, moth stupid.

Sitting in cornfields you should tell stories. Oh yes, little, gentle stories, to bring a smile. Great big bigger than life stories with characters loud and bright, with noises, jokes, colour. Who should tell it. An old man with wisdom cut deep into the lines of his face. Cut with pain, beauty. Storyteller's eyes, steady as a heartbeat, wild, acrobatic, bright, gentle. He'd been an aviator, flown transports out of Marseilles after the War. Grown up in the Blitz, French Mother gave him a lilt in his voice, still romantic under the button-up coat of an Englishman. It's a good story, old, sad.

"Now is not the time to mourn for the oceans are not deep enough to hold our tears. I heard a song. It was the song of the last Giant, wailing and echoing through the depths of the ..Atlantic... He sang of loneliness. We who do not know love, have not touched such cold depths. Our love is desire, and lust, and having. Getting and having. Our love is red with pain. The song of the last giant echoes the sounds of the sky, water and fire, elemental beauty. No stumbling words. We, the tongue tripped have no song. We are mute.

He sang of the first dawns, when time was young and the music of the giants filled the oceans. When there was air to breath, and the rivers did not run with blood of our wars and the sting of our chemicals. He sang of pain, wounds cut deep by our greed. We who do not know love. He sang of despair, that gifts are lost, and love is dead, and we who do not know love cannot grieve its death. He sang of love, in colours we have no eyes to see, with music we cannot hear. He sang of love and my heart burst with the beauty of his song. We who do not know love are empty."

I am Christ on a hot summer's day sitting in the cornfield, and I'm thinking about a girl. There was this girl. Not just any girl, softer than sensual, harder than puzzles. There was this girl and I loved her. I loved her not with hearts and flowers as the French do, nor the passion and pizza of the Italians. I loved her with the plain love of an Englishman, resolutely, steadily, quietly. Here are my socks neatly folded. It looks like rain again. I love you. That sort of thing. The English are always hidden, never what they seem. Sometimes I think we should all be librarians. Scratch the surface of a Frenchman you find a romantic. Scratch an Englishman, you find a librarian. This is not fair. We speak in such definites, so this or that. Dealing from a loaded deck. The same words round and round, and we wonder why we are alone. All this is not important, except that we spend too long mumble-muttering, tongue tied and tripping over our inadequate words.

I am an Englishman. Say it once or say it a thousand times. Each time a different Englishman in a different world. This time I am an Englishman who fell in love. Mine is a scruffy love. An old letter read so many times the tears and creases have become old friends. My love is odd socks, getting on the wrong train, a snowball fight, kicking around in leaves. Mine is the love that jumps in puddles, giggles, kisses in the rain, makes mistakes, tells bad jokes. Mine is the love that listens to her heartbeat in the silence of the night. These are the things that matter. We should talk more.

I am Christ on a hot summer's day sitting in the cornfield and I am crying, because we do not talk.

The Beautiful
Octopus Club

Tryptich

The Meeting (i)

The first thing I noticed
was he wouldn't look at me,
or even near me,
or even through me,

I'd been told what to expect
but this threw me
more than I expected,

"Can be challenging"
didn't quite cover it,
"He bites and smears himself in shit"
covered it,

He was seven,
I liked his mother right away
coped alone till he was five,
Dad had dived for cover soon after diagnosis,

Autism,

The weekend started badly
and got worse,
You can either wipe up shit or not,
Luckily and muckily I could,
Her first break in years,
My first "caring job"
ended in tears,

mine not his.

Walking in Rectangles (ii)

The garden was beautiful
full of interesting shrubs
and tubs of bedding plants,

The lawn was neat and mowed
but owed its oddness
to the rectangular path
worn down to earth and dust,

I watched him as he trod it,
thumb and two fingers of each hand
rubbing carefully selected blades of grass
held close to his face
as he paced his rectangle,

"Cannot communicate"
"non-verbal and aggressive",

I guess because I had nothing else to do
and I like to feel I'm
doing something,
I got up and followed him,

Two hours we trod the dusty rectangle
Two hours,
I even picked some grass and twidled,
two hours

and he turned

and he looked at me.

Piggy-back (iii)

Fourteen and awkward
and fancying Helen,

and wanting her to just know
I existed,

Sunday afternoon
Talja, (his mum was Norwegian),
spent four happy hours
(my happiness not his)
showing me each piece of lego
each scrap of paper,
each hidden piece of cutlery,
that was his world,

I had to touch each one
hold it close to my eyes,
and to my surprise
a whole new world
unfurled and breathed,

We went to the park
his lonely gait
a stark reminder that he
had not changed,

We took a different way home
came across a cattle grid,
incongruos somehow,
and how to cross,

I knelt and offered up my back
"Piggy back?"
and up he jumped,
and up he jumped
and I existed in his world,
and sometimes
this is
what love is,

Twenty-four and awkward
and trying to make friends
with a boy
from another world

Winston

Winston,
Jamaican dad
but he was always a south of the river lad,
Catford, New Cross, Lewisham,

"His grin could win the world cup of grins"
that was his Nan, tall and dark and beautiful,
She spoke at his funeral...
"Beautiful, also, is the sun
Beautiful, also, are the souls of my people"

She spoke not of the colour of his skin,
rich and dark like beauty,
she spoke of his disability,
autism,

His gift was that he learned to speak
our ordinary language,
his life a triumph of rich nights
spent singing with his band,
"Heart and Soul",

and he was their heart
and he was their soul,

and I know my words are too pale
to capture him,

but he was my friend,

Winston.

Hester

Hester wore hot-pants
that was her thing
in 1991
in Sydenham,

I was 24
in the middle of a year
of voluntary service
when I moved in,

Three bedroom terrace
but one spare
since Cynthia left,
Alzheimer's,

"You'll be ok,
but if she doesn't like you
your things are out the window
or sold at a boot fair"

I could not have loved her more
had she been my own sister;
hotpants
and downs syndrome,

and an attitude to life
that said
take me as I am
or leave me be.

Bernie

There aren't really words for Bernie
not really
just myths and stories
and knowing smiles;

Coming back from Alan's stag night
in the shopping trolley
and puking all over the night-staff
people with Downs Syndrome don't do that,
Bernie did;

Stealing spoons from wherever he went
hiding them in his underwear
to be revealed with a shout of "poons"
in the middle of some important social worker visit,
and laughing
like it was the best joke in the world,
and it was;

Hiding all the stuff of any new staff
all around the house
and looking so innocent
because he was blind;

Singing "Bend it"
by Dave Dee, Dozey, Beaky, Mick and Tich,
non-stop
till everyone gave up and joined in
and laughing
like it was the best joke in the world
and it was;

And that hoilday at Butlin's
when I had to share a double bed with him
because they got the booking wrong,
and he told me to behave;

And standing there
as best man at Alan's wedding

all suited up and booted
and showing all the respect and love
that they needed,
getting it
just right;

that was Bernie.

David

The first time I met David, he bit me.

I am standing outside the hospital, the old gates to the hospital, Victorian arches, that are lonely left, un-instituted, and substituted by modern housing, housing us, separately, Barrat-barracked solitude. David is with me, he stands near me, still nervous after twenty years away. Today is supposed to be a celebration. We've come to show him that Grove Park, that dark Victorian bedlam has gone. It is not a celebration. It is a dancing on graves, brave laughter of the survivors of the system, cystern pumped and thumped so many times it blunted, became blunt. We are blunt in our un-feeling, our oh so revealing blindness to what is right before our eyes, is wrong before our eyes.

The first time I met David, he bit me.

I am standing outside the hospital and I at least smile, my wry-dry-trying-to-be-empathetic-turning out pathetic smile. This is his pain not mine. I cannot borrow it to look good. I shouldn't even try, but I do. Twenty five years of ward-ridden bored-written boredom are his to forgive. He does not. He remembers the beatings and the rapes, the hunger and the hurt, the lies to his parents, when they came, if they came. We all hid him, hid from him, like that aunt you never spoke of, choked on the christmas cards your mother sent; poor recompence for the unvisited, the forgotten.

The first time I met David, he bit me and called me "nurse". He had a fear of tall men with glasses. The care plan said..."Autism is his world, you are the uninvited guest. Learn to speak his language".

I am standing outside the hospital, and David turns and takes my hand. He wants to leave, not touch me. I understand. We go. And that is the end of it. The taking of stock, the paying of debts for a social work system that never even knew. These are his pains, his wounds, and I am grateful they are his, to forgive, let go....or know forever.

The first time I met David, he bit me.

I can see why.

Sarah

"Make it stop, make them Beatles go away"
It's ok Sarah, they are gone now.

Sarah had her own lounge
in a care home for 32 people
all with "challenging behaviour"
she was "too violent" to risk mixing
with others
with us.

Sarah had Asperger's
but not the friendly face of it;
the lost in a nightmare world
of unfolding fears and tears
face of it.

Sarah's was a world
I could not access,
I could not place myself
in any framework that made any sense
to her,

I could not connect.

When you work in care
no-one tells you
how many funerals there will be
or how sometimes
you really
can't make it better.

Sarah, just once shook me
took me by surprise
looked into my eyes
and said....."make it stop".

I couldn't.

Autism is lonely, and terrifying,
and we need
to try harder.

"Make it stop, make them Beatles go away"
It's ok Sarah, they are gone now.

A Conversation With Kenneth

You know you're batting on a losing wicket
when the notes say...
"high functioning Asperger's with challenging behaviour"
all thoughts of being soft are wavered.

Kenneth rang rings round me
he seemed to understand the rules
but in the end
was too cool to succumb,

It is a hard lesson for staff
but laughingly well learned
"Learning Disability"
does not mean dumb.

Kenneth's logic was irrefutable
unmutable in its simplicity...

"I want to go to Chessington World of Adventures.
I can't so I am unhappy.
I am unhappy so I will...
cut all the power leads
turn on all the taps
flood all the rooms
and deflate all the tyres
on the staff's cars."

None of this was malice
just the odd logic-magic that can be autism.

He won, of course,
not blackmail, but a "managing of situations"
if the autism had allowed him humour
he would have laughed.

I smiled
for him and for myself
as we took the turning
marked "Chessington".

If you are going to talk,
walk that dodgy road,
be aware
that you are not
the most intelligent person
in a conversation
with Kenneth.

Down's Syndrome

I met Alan a week before his stag night
he invited me straight away, no questions,
he was like that,

The night itself was glorious, delirious,
we wheeled Bernie home in a shopping trolley,
he sang "Bend it"
all the way back to Forest Hill,

The wedding was thirty years of love
made real, special and ordinary,
everyone cried and smiled,
it was that sort of day,

Two years I was Alan's keyworker
best-mate-shirker and cup-of-tea-boy!
he called me slobberchops,
he knew,

The important stuff
the stuff about love and friends and all that,
the stuff I try to teach my kids
I learned from him,

His love was no less strong,
His tears were no less real,
His laughter was no less infectious,
because he had a label.

Park Bench

The old couple sit, park-benching,
he is tired,
she lets him rest
and they laugh at the ducks.

The holding of hands
is so gently done,
a putting on of gloves,
natural,
as only thirty years of love
can be.

I imagine them at parties;
her all flirty with wine
him, her rock, her safe place.
There is gentleness
in love.

I imagine them at home
arguing over EastEnders
or the football,
he gives in
and she cuddles up
on the sofa.

Passers-by stop and smile;
two people with Downs
giggling love
on a park bench.

I just see Chris and Alan,
an old married couple,
and I
smile too.

There is gentleness
in love.

Christine

Twenty years in Grove Park Hospital
walled in for the sin of having Down's...
Christine,

She married Alan, three years after
leaving that place,
a disgrace to our safe notions,
surely a scar on our emotions;
do we
really
represent
humanity?

She married Alan
and that should have said enough
gruff and grumpy voices
silenced by love.

She married Alan
having been his
partner-lover for twenty years or more;
(how we love that longevity today)

She married Alan
and two years later
was caring for...
a man robbed from her by Alzheimer's
a man robbed from her by hospitals
a man loved by her and given
a dignity in death,

by her.

My Favourite Holiday

Butlins at Bognor Regis
1992 and David.

This is David who hates change?
yes
This is David who bit you the first day you met?
yes
This is David with epilepsy
yes,
but not as bad as Jo's
And who else is going
Jo
You're fucking nuts,

Having cleared it with the Mrs. we set off for Butlins
four clients (David, Jo, Bernie and Dorothy)
two staff (me and Bridget)
for a week of tears and laughter
but mostly laughter,

David, autistic, never been away,
never had a holiday,
you don't get holidays from autism,

Jo, his girlfriend
in the sense that she clung to him
hung on him for comfort, loved him,

Dorothy,
if Down's syndrome had a political wing she led it,
My friends call me Dolly, you can call me Dorothy,

Bernie, this is not his story but he was there,

enough to say he could always make me laugh
just by saying "spoons",

First night was frightful, Jo had a major seizure in the dining hall
and all the guests just stared,
David got upset, very fretful
so I took him to the launderette and we watched the washing cycles
it comforted me as well.

The rest was just the best
the best of times,
David's smile at the fan dancers (not naked but he thought so)
Bernie watching the go-carts (he was blind but swore he saw them)
Jo just happy, no muttered words or scared looks,
Dorothy, my Dolly, relenting and giving me a cuddle
only to pour a puddle of coke down my back
how they all laughed at that,

But most of all David
he hadn't changed,
just been allowed to be in a different place
and watching his face I learned what that can mean.

Butlins at Bognor Regis
1992 and David,
my favourite holiday.

John

something dirty
something crushed
swept away
forgotten dust

I knew John for six years
and I don't remember him smiling.

I knew him first as "undiagnosed
with a non-specific learning disability".

I knew him as the one who lived alone
in a flat in Lee, "copes but needs help".

I knew him as the one with the porn collection
"no female staff will work with him".

I knew him as the one who listened to Dolly Parton
"because she has big tits and I think my mum liked her".

I knew him as a pedlar of petty drugs
and getting the charges dropped because of "his condition".

I knew him as the one who beat his mate up
'cos his mate's girlfriend said she'd been hit.

I knew him as the man who always wore a suit and tie,
but rarely shaved and never washed, just sprayed de-oderant.

I knew him as the friend who turned up drunk on tennants special brew,
at my flat, Christmas morning, puked in the sink
and made sure I was not alone that Christmas
because he knew Anita was away at home.

I knew him as the man, who only once
spoke about his family, that put him in care,
aged five, to be beaten and abused
till he could get out of "that fucking hole".

I knew John for six years
and I don't remember him smiling.

something dirty
something crushed
swept away
forgotten dust

on any other day

on any other day
i'd have gone to hospital
had the bites cleaned out
shouted at some nurse
whose fault it wasn't,
taken something
to numb the bruises.

on any other day
there would have been
no need to "get in the way"
but jamie had lost it
and there were family visiting.

on any other day
a soft word,
a kick-about in the garden,
nutella on toast,
would have calmed him,

but he was un-visited
ignored by a family
who'd rather pretend
he never existed,
at christmas.

on any other day
he might not have given
such a howl-driven picture
of his pain.
misunderstood.

anyone who thinks...
that being autistic means you have no emotions
that being autistic means you cannot connect
that being autistic means people don't matter to you
...please see with different eyes.

on any other day
i might have been angry
but i went home to my family
and shared christmas.

jamie.

Cynthia

I never knew Cynthia,
just the shell of her
moments of her that reminded others
who she was
with laughter
or tears,

She'd lived independently
with Hester,
for as long as anyone could remember
and then
she couldn't,

A Doctor once told me
that anyone with Downs
who lives past 50
has a 50/50 chance of getting Alzheimer's,

That Cynthia lived for five more years
when Alan died in five months
says what a stubborn, brave and
belligerent old thing she was
and must have been in her prime.

I never knew Cynthia
just the shell of her,
but she was beautiful
in her loss
and there were many times
as I fed her with a sippy cup
that she'd take a swing at me
and tell me she could
do it her bloody self.

Beautiful.

a different beauty

i've seen naked.

cynthia
fifty-two with a catheter fitted,
three years of alzheimer's
stole the sparkle
that comes with "downs",
cynthia -
i changed her pad
wiped away the shit
others chose not to smell
near the end of their shift,

cynthia
bed baths and hoists,
dignity
isn't measured on a tick list of pad changes,
but in the eyes
and in the days
when
naked moments
passed between us -

giving her a drink
in a sippy cup,
her lips, old and cracked,

life is brittle
and hurts,

she just left me
no words
no fuss,

she wasn't family
but important;
fragile.

cynthia.

Rose

Rose - *undiagnosed non-specific learning disability*
Rose - *extreme challenging behaviour*
Rose - *verbally abuse and uncooperative*

Rose, by any other name would be as beautiful.
It was not till four years after I stopped working with her
that I realised she had Tourette's, but I would bet
she didn't care what it was called.

I was her keyworker for two years
two years of arguing about her meds,
of banging our heads together
and coming out the other side non-the-wiser.

Her obsessive-compulsive behaviours
were seen as "challenges"
and I was too new to know better,
so I bought into that.

Her family were great,
three sisters who all related well
and knew just how to calm her
with a word or two.

That day she threw the TV through the window
at 52 and petite I was impressed,
It made a satisfying mess
from two floors up.

That holiday on the Norfolk Broads
not one swear word the whole week,
I think rivers have some secret magic
that speaks to who we are.

I left her in '93
but saw her five years later,
She smiled and knew my name
somehow that made it worse, my absence.

Rose - mis-diagnosed and lost
in a system where errors cost
real pain.

Richard

Richard is not a poem.
He is an ugly abuse,
used and discarded
hard to like,
and harder to work with,
ugly as life can be.

Richard is not a poem.
He is an abuser,
taught from an early age
but still...
unforgiven.
difficult to cope with.

Richard is not a poem.
He is the man
who threatened staff with a knife
who threatened staff with a smile,
who talked about arson;
because he knew that burns the system.

Richard is not a poem,
he was abused in care
and dare we say that how he
responded
is wrong
is anything other than normal,

Richard is not a poem
and I do not like him
and I never did,
and is that
how we
treat the weak?

Glen

It was a dirty night
Railway Tavern, Sydenham,
1991.

It was a dirty pool-playing
lock-in of a night.

Me and Glen played doubles
took on allcomers
anyone and everyone
any shape or size
we didn't care.

Glen always asked for two shots to one
on account of his Downs,
on account of his big soft eyes
and winning smile,
people learned fast
he'd only sneak that one past newcomers.

If I'd been with anyone else...
as Glen fleeced the punters with side bets,
If I'd been with anyone else...
as Glen took the piss with trick shots,
If I'd been with anyone else
I'd have been lucky to escape a beating,
but I honestly think they saw it
as giving to charity,
and I was with Glen;
Glen who anyway
would probably
have thrown the first punch.

It was a dirty night in Sydenham
in a fag-end dog-rough pub
and it was magic.

Kenny

Kenny was a mate of mine,
we used to go and watch Millwall together
managed to blag a couple of season tickets
on account of his disability
I went along as his carer;
too bloody funny.

Kenny had Down's Syndrome.
He didn't worry about it;
he had some trouble speaking
and the most evil sense of humour I ever knew
I can still hear his laugh
worse than Mutley.

Kenny swore a lot
but
"Fuck off" came out "Fug all".
He was proud that he could say his own name,
properly,
H
he'd tap his chest and say
"Kenny Evans" when introduced.

I didn't know better when I first met him
so I tapped my chest and said..."Philbrook, Simon Philbrook..."
He roared with laughter
and ever after when I arrived he'd tap me on the chest saying..
"Fug-all, Fug-all, Smime"
then fall about laughing.
I miss that.

Kenny loved football,
he loved the cheering and the chants,
and anyone who scored.....them or us!
Upper tier behind the goal
whenever "the referee's a wanker" could be heard
you knew that Kenny would be standing up conducting
like it was last night of the proms.

At home to some crap nobody's in the cup
Thatcher steps up to head away a corner
perfect own goal
silence,
visitors end was always empty then,
Kenny stands up
shouts "GOAL" in perfect diction,
I couldn't look.
then from a couple of rows behind the chant began
"Stand up if you love Kenny.....Stand up if you love Kenny".
He conducted'
I cried.

This is why I bloody love football.

Hugo

I woke at just gone 2am
the on-call phone
nagging me towards
a bleary hello,

"There's been a break-in
someone's stolen the Christmas Tree"

I gathered my thoughts
and considered how
two waking night staff
could not see a thief break in
and steal an eight foot Christmas tree
from the main lounge
of a care home with 32 people in it.

Hugo.

I threw on some clothes
and drove the five miles in,
begining to rehearse
the words to use,
some sharp abuse
for losing Christmas.

Hugo.

Have you called the police,
rhetorical of course,
of course they hadn't,
a procedures file is often considered
as irrelevant when it comes down to it.

Hugo.

I brushed past the staff and went straight up
to Hugo's room
and there
squashed in the corner

was an eight foot Christmas Tree,
I smiled.

Hugo was a short, fierce, Down's man
with a beautiful ponytail
and a sense of the absurd.

He stole anything he could
and destroyed anything he couldn't steal.

This was his masterpiece,
an eight foot tree past two staff
up three floors along a corridor
and put back up
squashed, but decorated.

The man was obviously
a genius
and I could only smile.

The staff at least had the decency
to muster sheepish looks.

Hugo
that night
and forever
my hero.

Mud on a Sunday Morning

You don't know how good mud feels
till you are sat in it
exhausted from laughter
on Boxing Day morning
in Crystal Palace Park,

Jumpers as goalposts
Bernie in goal at one end
Hester at the other
Only two rules...
staff are not allowed to score
and anyone showing too much skill
has a penalty against them,

No-one could stay on their feet
and no-one could remember the score
in the pub by mid-afternoon.

Ten years later
I am sat in a meeting
with social workers who have never even met
the service user they are reviewing,
I am speaking fluently
in the language of a Registered Care Home Manager,
and I wonder
where all the mud went.

The sky is a great big green balloon

Me and Johnathan
sit quietly
looking at the sky
top of Primrose Hill,
London, all still and whispered before us,
just as I imagined it
from the movies.

Visited his mum
now eighty
the weight of years
paint-peeled and dusty
across her face,
but traces of laughter
still lingered.

The journey up,
from south of the river
had been a nightmare,
the tube tugged hard
at his ticks and tricks
touching any cornered edge
to feel safe.

"They never called it autism
when he was a kid"
his mum had said,
"Just beat him and told me
he was simple".

"He never really talked,
that's how I knew,
at first I thought he caught it
from no knowing his Dad,
died at Tabruk you know,
I have a medal"

"Later I saw that he was lost
somewhere in there.

There have been moments...
he'll catch your eye
and say something, and smile.
I know he loves me".

I lie back in the grass
passing time to let the rush hour go
before we show our faces to the journey.
Johnathan looks up, then half across at me and says
"The sky is a great big green balloon",
I look up
and see it just the same,
"Yes it is" I say.
Yes it is.

The Beautiful Octopus Club

who are my people?
where do i belong?

I'm going down to Deptford
the Albany
first Wednesday of the month
"The Beautiful Octopus Club",

I'm going to be there
with my friends
back to my roots
hoots of laughter,
and Winston's grin,

draped from the ceiling,
each tentacle
a miracle of colour,
this is the place
I smile most,

dodgy disco
decks the evening out
with awful dancing
and laughter,

Pauline sidles idly up to the d.j.
says she loves him
and requests Cliff Richard
we all groan,

Cynthia is here
in her wheelchair
eyes light up
as "The Young Ones" blares out,
"Shout" follows quickly
and we're all dancing,

Winston takes the mike
mighty lungs ready

heart and soul,
he sings,
"Heart and Soul" the best band
in the world,

Kenny starts to pogo,
I still don't know
where he learnt that,
batters into
a couple of the "care workers",
evil grin
and he begins again,
like it's 1977,

Hester's wearing hotpants
of course,
"The Beautiful Octopus Club"
tub-thumping happiness,

I'm going down to Deptford
the Albany
first Wednesday of the month,
to be with my friends,

these are my people
this is where i belong.

Fly Posters Will Be Prosecuted

Time: 1937

tick tock
     tick tock
          tick tock
     tick tock
tick tock

the calm before...

there are no words for "after"
just tears
and guilt
humanity will never take the next great step forward until it recognises,
understands, accepts and confronts the motivation that led to the
holocaust

appeasement;
such an ugly word
a looking the other way
a deliberate blindness
a shame that still haunts,

gather up,
gather up
in the arms of your pity
those who expect
no love from above

never again
       never
         again
againagainagainagainagainagainagainagainRWANDA

"but they're only natives, they don't know better, would never happen in
europe"

would never happen
                never happen
                        happen
                                in europe;
                                        in bosnia
TICK TOCK, TICK TOCK, TICK TOCK, TICK TOCK, TICK TOCK,
who will stop this fucking clock
whose head upon the block
will shock (machete shock)
enough
to
stop,

one voice speaks for six million; the voice not of a sage or a poet but of an ordinary little girl

Time: 1937
Anschluss & Poland
just waiting

the voice of one child
is still
all,

will still
all,
we need to listen;

TICK TOCK, tick tock, tick tock, tick tock, tick tock...

my favourite shirt

my favourite shirt
is a poem.

i put it on
when going out
to "smart places"
black tie.

my favourite shirt
is brushed cotton
and needs cuff-links

i have a pair
of Homer Simpson ones
showing
his big yellow hairy arse.

my favourite shirt
has a wank-stain

on the front at the right
just below the spare button
(i have never used a spare button
i just buy a new shirt),

my favourite shirt
is a poem

i love it when i'm wearing it
but honestly
a good fuck
is better than poetry.

fly posters will be prosecuted

muslim students with rucksacks
will not be sat next to on trains,

young blacks will be stopped
and searched,

children will be driven to school
in four-by-fours,

gays will be beaten
and jews will be spat at,

men will fuck whoever they can
and lie to their wives,

politicians will smile
and kiss babies,

the homeless will die on the streets
when the weather turns,

prostitutes will take crack
and executives will take cocaine,

targets on CO_2 emissions
will be talked about,

footballers will get away with rape
and drunk driving,

mcdonalds will sell burgers
and starbucks will sell coffee,

fly posters
will be prosecuted,

this is england
have a nice day.

In Memory of Me

Light the ovens,
Burn to ash
The race that would deny me,
Do this in memory of me

Defend the oil,
Boil alive the pagans
On the road from Al Jahra
Do this in memory of me

Reign Supreme,
Prepare the beams from which to hang
Your strange fruit
Do this in memory of me

Suffer the children,
Teach the beatings into them
Our little secret,
Do this in memory of me

Worship me
I don't care how you live
Or what you give, just make it dollars,
Do this in memory of me.

apply in writing

energetic female seeks reluctant male for post grad project,
esoteric interest in lawnmower starter motors an advantage,

north american country seeks symbol of redemption,
previous experience not required (equal ops employer)

elderly female seeks weekend companionship,
KY supplied, socks not a problem, no timewasters,

13 year old crack head seeks 40+ male for cash
all tricks considered, anal extra, ford mondeo preferred,

comic enthusiast seeks copies 7 thru 16, 2000AD, also ring gift
from issue one, phone me (not wednesdays takes mother to bingo)

artist seeks life models, unusual body shapes preferred,
please send photos, PO BOX only, cash paid,

TV station seeks contestants for reality show
dysfunctional personality essential, apply in writing.

The long night of the homosexual elephants

"Our ambition should be to rule ourselves, the true kingdom for each one of us; and true progress is to know more, and be more, and to do more." Oscar Wilde

The night of the homosexual elephants we drew out our sharp knives and waited in the dark alleys. Piccadilly was a no go, so we congregated in Soho and Jez whipped the crowd up to a frenzy. We saw a few film stars, out slumming it and enjoying the fireworks. There were others, politicians scurrying home after getting their cocks sucked by an odd assortment of tranvestites, dykes, hookers and tramps.

The night of the homosexual elephants belonged to the people. We rose up and wiped away all the mutha-fucking shit we were scared of. We rose up and cut the fucking elephants to pieces. The fires were lit all over London and we ate out on their sorry carcasses, all that sweet crackling, their flesh tasted like chicken and we broke the windows of Tesco Express to get some dark soy sauce, and a few cans of cheap cider.

The night of the homosexual elephants was glorious. The whores all gave it up for free, to celebrate the death of so many elephants; and those that didn't we took anyway, because we were the new gods. We were life that night, fire-bright and fierce. We were the gods of the old testament bringing our wrath down on the homosexual elephants. They made us sick in our abhorrence, and we cut them down.

The night of the homosexual elephants will go down in history. The night the homosexual elephants were finally punished for their evil abhorrent behaviour. They have brought the punishment of the baby lord jesus down upon us. They have brought global warming and tsunamis. They destroyed New Orleans. They flew into the twin towers.

My tutor once told me that to study, to "eat an elephant" you had to take it one bite at a time. The night of the homosexual elephants was our first juicy bite and their blood runs down our jowls so sweetly. They are succulent in their depravity.

The night of the homosexual elephants I wore my white hood and I burned my cross

The night of the homosexual elephants......is coming.

Recognising the smell of shit

I sit down and decide to write a shit poem
so shit that everyone has to say
"jesus this is shit"
and i start writing
sitting in the backroom
of an irish pub in Boyce Street
and then this girl walks in
all split skirt and legs
and suddenly i'm thinking of a poem by bukowski.
Yeah i see you, charles bukowski
sitting at your californian race track
eyeing up young legs
and guessing which horse
might just come in at 40-1
and laughing at me
and all the stupid-fucking-dimwit-poets
like me
who spend so long with their heads up their own arse
that they are no longer able
to recognise the smell of shit.

imagine

When he was five
my son fell over running
tumbling on the hard concrete of the playground
I turned around, thinking it someone else's child,
Imagine my fear,

Imagine the sound
of a baton cracking a skull
dull thumps
clumps of brain
splattering freshly creased uniforms
and monks robes
and students satchels
and the street,
Imagine the shit stinking prison
breathe it in,
skin peeled back
to get the pain right in,
Imagine it,
Imagine 9/11
all of them lined up
and shot,
one by bloody one
in front of you,
3000 is a low estimate for Burma 1988,
Imagine this happening again
and the silence
Imagine winning an election with eighty percent of the vote
then spending the next seventeen years under "house arrest"
and the silence,
Imagine there's no heaven
some days it's so, so easy,

My son was fine
imagine my relief.

London road

the pogues
dirty old town
cowley club PA system
london road

my friend vanessa
scores some gear
back of richer sounds
she'll be dead soon

out back in the bystander
latte and a fag
the last place in brighton
you can smoke

tommy's on the street again
can of special brew
and his three legged dog
both stink of piss

steve says you can get a blow job
in the toilets on the level
for the price of a ten bag
if you're not fussy

sirens break the cold
november night
crack house above the subway
closes early

some drunk got kicked to death
gutter left
back of the old wollworth building
something to do with a girl

it's always something to do with a girl.

unreliable witness

when i was at college
learning history, made up by historians,
yearning to get laid
more often than
just a drunken friday fumble,
i lived above a chippy,

hippy curtains said student digs
pig of a landlord
lorded it over us
for weekly rent,
half spent in midweek pub-crawls,

my innocence was befriended
by the local toms,
how wrong we are
about people,

my obvious unskilled need
made me appealing,
and their revealing outfits
were
hard
to ignore,

they joked about
how crap
i would be in bed
if i ever got there,
"teach you a thing or two
big boy!!!!"
they laughed

and i made friends with kylie,
younger than me
but knew more history
than dusty books,
one look at a punter
told her
what sort of cunt he was,

kylie (not her real name)
walked the mile
that was the Derby Road,
fat bald pimp
too wimpy to protect her
when she got done over
one night,

pigs were curb crawling
drooling and fawning over scanty flesh
and happened to mesh
the fucker
who fucked her
up,

middle class, middle aged, magistrate
instead of castrating him
threw it out
of court
of course,

unreliable witness.

Timeline

This is a long time ago.
I am trying to sleep at my grandparents' house.
I hear his gurgled cough all night.
I don't worry.

This is now.
I am caressing the sweat off my daughter's headcold.
I am the one they quietly cuddle up to.
I worry.

This is later.
I am visiting my brother in hospital.
I heard the words on the news, now I feel them, dirty bomb.
I listen to his cough, and remember my grandfather.

what will survive of us...

the old brickwork
shivvered away the remains of painted love
"jezz does helen"
rained and blistered, faded,
years after they forgot
those clumsy moments,

the school wall crumbles,
slowly arthritic joints
need repointing,
but are lost
on some crumpled list,

the last scratching,
etched and chiseled
by metal ruler, and adolescent earnest,
"kev4jen
4ever"

what will survive of us
is ciggy stubs
graffiti
and half remembered
blow jobs.

I am a wanker

I didn't know what masturbation was till I was sixteen
My parents, being English,
imagined
that if it wasn't talked about it didn't exist,
they had a point
but some fucker could have told me,

I'd heard the words
and laughed on cue at smutty innuendo
but never really knew,

and then kapow!
and how!

and then jenny
(names have been changed to protect the innocent)
jenny who showed me, taught me, teased and pleased me,
jenny who knew that wanking is just great,

she waited till we'd dated for a month or so
and then (me twenty-one her twenty)
she let go her secrets,
"there is no shame in sex"
cannot be taught
it must be bought through experience
through girls (or boys) who are
jenny-perfect,

she stripped us naked
and demanded I wank
show her how I "crank it off" (laughter)
and then she showed me
and I can't think of anything
more intimate
more revealing
more sexually beautiful
than what she taught me,

and now
when someone calls me
a stupid wanker
it is "stupid" I object to.

nearly a love song

i woke
to "Born Slippy"
thumping up
from downstairs,
cheap Gite
in St. Malo,

couldn't think
where she was
tossed blankets lay around
then the sound
of bacon frying,

love
is a pile of shit
but
i'll stay with someone forever
who makes me bacon butties
the morning after.

Pele's Dummy

I had this girlfriend once
Loved her to bits
Gorgeous tits, nasty temper,
She went away, Cambridge,
Rainy days waiting for trains,
She studied law
Bored the arse off me
so I spent my time
admiring hers,

I met her at the bar one night
She greeted me with a kiss,
Soft, and just lingering enough
to make me think I hadn't seen
the subtle brush against the hand
of some bloke stood next to her,
No point rowing
When you're not sure.

Years later
Waiting for a bus in New Cross,
Lazily shop window gazing
HD ready TV's,
Brazil 1970....Team of the Century
On loop,
Pele's dummy on the Italian keeper
used his body, the way he ran,
to send the poor sod the wrong way,

Skill and speed of thought
Beyond the imagination of the ordinary,

You have to admire that,
And her arse.

bad news

"bad news always reminds me of you"
danny, (one shit short of a brickhouse)
but you didn't mess with him,
luckily
he knew my brother,

"we always lose when i fucking see you"
danny again, (and technically true)
and i didn't want to argue,
friendly
pre-season games don't count,

"if we lose today you're fucking dead"
danny, (you have to love him)
wasn't subtle, brutal but fair,
apparently
I left before the half-time whistle, 3-0.

paraffin and perfume

we all laughed when the match came up,
some old tramp
who signed up for a cup of tea
smelled of paraffin and wee,
had the marrow
needed,
took three cops to find him,
dumpster ducking in an alley
thought he was in trouble,
pee'd himself
stank the car out,

washed and scrubbed up
looked like my grandad,
glad to help
for a few nights
of hospital respite,
daisy,
daddy's delightful little perfume princess
got better,
the old guy
died in the cold snap that winter,
sometimes
that's just the way it goes.

Blood Oranges

halls of residence, 1985
sat next to the quiet irish girl, val,

lunch was something messy
supposed to be italian
not even close
then apples
or blood oranges,

she just started crying
no warning
no meaning to it,

i leant my shoulder
while i looked around
embarrassed
for her friends,

walked her back to her rooms
hugged me
fiercely,
confused,
but I knew enough
to kiss her back
hard,

she stood back
and undressed
button after button
i have tasted few moments so beautiful,
so erotic,

later i discovered
that her cousin
had been shot in the head
left dead on the falls road
by orangemen,

we never spoke of it
or much at all,
and i feel sad
that we will always have
such different memories
of blood oranges.

decade

i am pissing blood. i am pissing blood into a dirty toilet bowel, kidneys all fatty with burgers, liver fucked with the cirrhosis of reading too much bukowski. yes i'll have fries with that. the kids from next door are smoking on the street corner. our children will hate us. they must. not for simple lack of trust, or wanks disturbed, but for all the lies we hide behind, keep score would ya and choose the ones to make the cut; the tooth fairy, santa claus, and jesus; muhammed, yahweh, krishna all the lot; even here our own-sown lies deceive us, we just can't see that we are all we've got in this sad, cold life, and when we are through sorting tin cans from paper to save the planet, as we drive the mile to school to pick them up, it's clear, the lies are there to see. our children will hate us; they must, for we have turned their world to empty dust, slowly.

i am pissing blood. the blood of the new and everlasting covenant, conveniently forgetting the lie (why bother with small details). a man wearing a dress, incanting spells and dishing out blood and flesh does it for me. star trek - the next generation. captain kirk speaks mandarin and has no truck with sex and all that brings. he will abstain from mucky rendezvous and alien fucks, for the greater glory of the people's republic. i'll guess at one more decade till china will rule the world, the subtle irony of clearing up the mess we made of it. all the shit we have spewed into the air. toxins we have dumped underground, additives of every sort that run through our food without permission, not a sound of contrition when caught, hands in the till of our future; our children pay the bill.

i am pissing blood. i am pissing the blood of my friends. i am pissing the blood of the labelled. disabled. mental handicap. spastic. loon. learning disability. utility words to keep them at bay, away from our lives. i am pissing their blood and it is no less red. their love is just as sharply felt, their hate as fierce, their touch as soft, as though it matters what imperfect hand is dealt to them, to any, we are not perfect but we are beautiful in all our tears, in all our imperfections. our defects are our beauty. humanity is near to being bankrupt if it cannot love the weak, the poor, the ugly "less", who are the whole of us, and is it not enough that they must learn to love these hard-won scars without us picking at them till they puss. our schadenfreude. grateful it's not us.

i am pissing blood. the blood of the lonely. i am one of you. prozac nation filled by strange equations of balancing need with pills. don't bother listening, just tick repeat prescription. love, love is not blind, we are blind, we see the waste of human detritus and think to medicate it away. set it free. let it be felt, this squalid lonely stink of pain. SET IT FREE that we may show real love, none of us are above loneliness, none of us are free from the fear that steals away all hope. we can only confess to being human, to being alone through the cold night that we call life. you look at me and want me to condone these pills, this indolence, this lack of strife towards the simple truth that we fail to see, despair is love, made real in you, and me.

i am pissing blood, the blood of the moon, all rich with life, vibrant in your whispered reds. the very blood of life, beauty. beauty you are woman, not in the curve of your breasts or the fullness of your lips. you are beauty in the spirit, the verve with which you throw yourself at all life's trips and pitfalls. beauty you are woman through eyes age-wearied in their love and breasts made rich in the suckling. and those that know will see the beauty, truth that does not fade or grey in the eyes of man; woman you stand tall and fierce with eyes of fire, with all the desire of sex crackling through your touch, and i hear the aching call of eyes, and your lips are just soft enough to remind me that what we are, is love.

i am pissing blood with broken glass, each shard a sharp reminder of the pain we have made. i am pissing the blood of the broken whore, crack-fetid and congealing as it leaks from her nose across the floor, token efforts of paramedics can't stem its flow, crimsoning a shit-stinking rest room, in a piss-stinking bar, in a dead-eyed city. the beauty of people dies too soon, and we let it die, whimpered and un-cried. "gather up in the arms of your pity, the sick, the depraved, the desperate, the tired, all the scum of our weary city". gather them up, hold them and learn to see the beauty that they are, for they are us, in our desperate lonely ugliness.

i am pissing blood and it is my blood. my words. my hopes and fears. my humanity and i am ugly. beautifully ugly.

A Georgia Moon at Midnight

wordplay

the tired sun unblouses into dusk
and musky apple-blossomed night
lights tender moons, and fireflies
describe the gentleness
of such
quiet
moments

Haiku

Winter calls me,
Sharp, unspoken, ice-glazed words;
This is not love.

Georgia Moon at Midnight

i am unslept
through this dusky-warm night

like blues and whisky
i hear the breath of new orleans

like softness, i ache for you,
quietly,

an un-made bed,
a smile, a touch,

these are what i miss
this georgia night.

not a love poem

I love you like pooh
as rich as shit
my love for you
squelching in it,

I love you like potatoes
gone all knobbly
my sometimes chipped, or mashed,
or wobbly, love for you,

I love you like teacups
all smashed on the floor
that temper of yours
I adore,

I love you like melons
your breasts of course
I cannot resist them
they give me a hard-on,

I love you like farts
and the laughter imparted
when you score mine out of ten,
who could not love that?

who could not love you.

the list of things you'll only do once

some moments are unique
tweak your memories and they fade
jaded by repetition,

losing my virginity, oh god,
honestly, don't make me remember
a fumbled tumbled relief..."at least that's out the way",

going to my grandmother's funeral
unusual weather is all I remember
tears and rain and tears...just muddled,

posing for the life drawing class
some arse I lost a bet to made me, and yet,
you know it kind of turned me on,

that abseil horror, and I hate heights,
but somehow found myself
two hundred feet high...why?

that first kiss with her,
love is nothing
until you've kissed the one

some things
don't come around
often.

Solitary Sunday

The solitary sunday
bumbles its way around the room
but no one notices,

The solitary sunday
forgets to do the washing up
but no one complains,

The solitary sunday
ignores the TV and sits quietly
just remembering,

Sometimes
solitude
comforts.

Old Poets Never Die...

Old poets never die
they lie about on bookshelves
in the library
all musty
and smelling of incontinence,

They haunt us through classrooms
with their anapestic
oft-dactylic
whispers,

They mug us with sestinas
on dark nights
when we wander lonely
through drunken streets
taking a short-cut
back from that reading,

They operate on us
in local hospitals
with their sharp scalpelled words
and lack of proper hygiene,

They refuse us credit
or turn down our social security claim
aiming to play beatniks tricks
on the unsuspecting young,

Old poets never die
they lie in wait
drinking the whisky out of our
grey polished lives,

waiting to show us
who's really best.

Bookmark

I love the smell of charity shops
of lives lived
just the wrong side of odd
that collection of pope john paul thimbles
still boxed,

I love the clothes
the jackets that even the homeless
would not dare wear,
the plastic slip on shoes
shouldering for space
next to re-souled brougues
with mis-matched laces,

But most
I love the books
the little inscriptions
dust-leaved but poignant
"To remember Auntie Fay
from Jim",

I found a photo once
tightly tucked
bookmarking
between the covers
Thomas Hardy - Poetry,

A woman's face
a smile
drew me to some place
lost,

Three words only
on the back
"Always yours, Alice"

I wondered at her life
of who she loved
and who misplaced

this tiny bookmark of her life,

I wondered what marks
will be left
by me,

I reshelved it gently
it seemed
quietly
proper.

cyanide blues

everyone said
his death
was very
out of character

fastidious
in most things
(shirts by van huesen
ties always double windsor)
the blunt
rusty
razor blades
were
incongruous

cyanide
sipped through pimms
with a slice of cucumber
would have been
more
elegant

depressing
how standards
have
slipped.

dead car river

he sat
riverbottomed
confused

like that bit in highlander
when he doesn't
drown

choose life
& the trainspotting toilet scene
flashed across his mind

he smiled
wry and absurd
like life

knowing that ewan mcgregor
will never
make a better film

schadenfreude
is such
delicious pleasure

undrowned
he shrugged
and open-windowed to the surface

perhaps fishfingers for tea
but sainsbury's on the way home
ketchup.

the mersey

sold,

river-soft-songs
do not
unsing your slavery,
do not
unshackle your pain,

from the liverpool docks
to the coast of antigua,

england sailed its ships
with a good wind
with a kind god,

empire...
an ugliness
a teaching
a reaching
of greed,

an emptiness,

empire...
a greatness
of britain,

a scar,

the blood mixes down the mersey
down the mersey and back again,
from Kingston to Birkenhead
from Port Antonio to Knowsley,

we are of one blood,
but,
we are not brothers
we are not friends,

we tell our wives
the same lies,
kiss our children
with the same love,
work the same tired hours
and live the same tired lives,

the old mersey
muddies us
mixes us in love and life and pain,

and slowly
we see
we are
the same,

both of us
made beautiful
in this
old river's
song.

Original Message

----------------- Original Message -----------------
From: **Room 101 Poetry**
Date: 21 Aug 2008, 16:02

Dear Sir/Madam,

We are a small poetry publishing company
that specialises in the online variety,

We are delighted to inform you of selection
in our upcoming poetry collection,

Please call the following off-peak-premium line
to confirm inclusion before there is no time,

0898-poetry-hotline

----------------- Reply Message -----------------
From: **Poet**
Date: 21 Aug 2008, 17:02

Dear "Poetry-helpline-we're-sorry-all-our-operatives-are-busy-please-
hold-we-value-your-call"

I selected option 1 for information regarding publication but was put on
hold.
I selected option 2 for help with particularly difficult rhymes, but was
put on hold again, and again, and again, when I got through I was told
to try "again".
I selected option 3 for prosody.....but the service was deleted years ago.
I selected option 4 for general inquiries and spent just under three

minutes listening to Helga-from-Sweden-reads-poetry-naked, maybe just over three minutes.
I selected option 5 for billing enquiries, and hung up straight away.

Thanks you for your consideration, but I shall wait until after my death for my genius to be recognised.

Poet.

Riverboating

Riverboating, summerfloating days
the heat hazed blue-blue Mississipi sky,
untying our knotted fears
uncrying our worries
in its deep muddy love,

Low-necking, cotton summer-dressing days
we weren't in love just very happy,
stealing coolness
from the softness of the river
its slow gentle love,

Paddlesplashing steamboat lovin' days
we laughed as kids
in our knee-scraping-huck-finn easy ways
in our scruffy friendship
we heard the river calling,

Riverboating, steamboat-whistle days
the heat hazed blue-blue Mississipi sky,
untying our knotted fears
uncrying our worries
in its deep muddy love,

in its soft slow love.

visiting the old house

it is a dusty sadness
all reds
and yellows

pale and peeling
in empty rooms

we are un-homed
now
no-one to hear us

faint light
through a crack in the door
is just a memory
of another day

those cobwebs

that gate needs fixing

this is not home.

My favourite poets

Kenneth Wolstenholme,
for me it begins with him, that undimmed line
you know the one,
I was not yet one when he spoke it,

Martin Tyler,
always eloquent, an Arsenal fan but
I listened to him find joy, give joy,
in that Giggs goal, in that semi-final,

Clive Tyldesley,
always under-rated
cup replays at Doncaster, who does those,
and then Istanbul, he believed and his words made me believe,

Brain Moore,
never "Motty" but nearly,
to be the next best poet of your generation must be cruel,
Arsenal '89 was his though and that was something,

Alan Green,
never seen but heard through crackling radios of youth
truth is his currency, and how,
and I love him for it,

Barry Davies,
his unwavering love of beauty holds him high
he saw it in that second Maradona goal
and to lose to such beauty is not such defeat,

And then...
John Motson,
poet of his generation, poet of our time,
my time, he grew me up with words
absurdly wrong sometimes but so perfect
always,
he gave me Owen's goal
and Pearce's penalty
and he gave me Ole Gunnar Solskjaer

winning it for Manchester
winning it for me
that second corner,

These are my poets
without them it is twenty two men
kicking a bag of air
who would care?

Bouleversement

bou•le•ver•se•ment
n.
1. A violent uproar; a tumult.
2. A reversal.
[French, from Old French bouleverser, to overturn : boule, ball (from Latin bulla) + verser, to overturn (from Old French, from Latin vers--re, frequentative of vertere, to turn).]

1983
me
seventeen
and spotty,

wore a sweat shirt
naff then
cool now,
retro makes no sense to me,

sat down with flat lemonade
and soggy crisps
to watch
THE BIGGEST FUCKING GAME OF FOOTBALL EVER!

in my little, awkward,
gentle, life,

we started well (Smith 1-0)
then fell behind (Stapleton and Wilkins 2-1)
then stevens (there's only one Gary Stevens 2-2)
then smith....

there's seconds left
he's through on goal
one kick and Brighton win the FA CUP,
"and smith must score"....the commentator roars,

we scream at the TV
like it can hear us

like we make the difference
like it is our glory, our moment,

it finishes 2-2
we lose the replay
four nil
"and smith must score",
bouleversement,
a violent uproar; a tumult,
a reversal,
indeed.

Night Bus

There's room here for everybody
He said, fatly-arsed sitting on the night bus,
Trussed-up-tight little girls giggle
as some spotty kid picks spots and oozes puss,

A tramp-like night-type drinker dribbles,
The bumps of sudden brakes not waking him,
A vamp-like goth-dressed woman wriggles
Wished she'd not gone commando...itchy skin,

A booted-suited sartorial-sharpened skin-head
Puts headphones on to drown out incessant din
Of dim-wit wittering drunk kids playing grown-ups
Who've mixed their red bull lights with cheap priced gin,

The driver sighs, just one more week till day shifts
Agreed to nights to pay for some school trip
The kids don't know how much he hates these wankers
Who treat him like some tiny piece of shit.

Zack-attack

The corridor
empty as only hospitals can be,
I waited, not my turn, not my child.

His size was the shock,
Twenty four weeks is not a lot of life
but he had little locks of hair,

And the tubes, everywhere,
and the beeping monitors
and the worried glances,

Zack, my nephew, a tiny little sack of trouble
later we called him "Zack-attack"
because he does,

Born dead (for nine minutes) tick tock, tick tock,
someone should have told him he was dead
would come as quite a shock,

And every night, for weeks the tired drive,
the tired fights to see who went,
to see if he would live another day, preparing always,

And now he's four
trouble could have no other name,
untamed spirits......

.....are meant to live..

A Summer in the Tarn Valley

sun and sadness
long, slow, beaten sadness,
of this road
without you

at seventeen
in between exams
i spent the summer
south of france
entranced,

old farmhouse gite,
eight friends, ending friendships,
not wanting to let go,

cheap red wine and crusty bread,
last supper, every supper,

we swam
in the warm pools
of the Tarn,
meandered moments
and warm rain,

six girls
and me and nat,
and not a thought
of sex and that,

sitting
stone-skimming
river-breathing
talking,

i mention this
not in passing,
but in thinking
of you,

to let you know
you are
my summer in the Tarn Valley,
and i miss you,

sun and sadness
long, slow, beaten sadness,
of this road
without you

recipe for wormburgers

go to garden
dig up worms
add to mince in blender
pinch of salt
shape and cook burger
serve to low-life brother-in-law who cheated on my sister but she
forgave him
enjoy rest of bar-b-que

Firestarter

I burn things
little tingles in my fingers
as I scratch the matches
slowly
against the roughened side,
enticing it
to lighten my mood.

I burn things
poems mostly
but I did once manage a short story,
the curling, blistering, satisfaction,
it's not that I'm after perfection
but the flicker-tickering attraction
of the yellow-red dance
makes me smile.

Songlines

Woman

Beauty, you are woman, not in the curve
of your breasts or the fullness of your lips;
you are beauty in the spirit, the verve
with which you throw yourself at all life's trips
and pitfalls. Beauty you are woman through
eyes age-wearied in their love and breasts made
rich in the suckling, and those that know
will see the beauty, truth that does not fade
or grey in the eyes of man. Woman you
stand tall and fierce with eyes of fire, with all
the desire of sex crackling through
your touch, and I hear the aching call
of eyes, and your lips are just soft enough
to remind me that what we are, is love.

Alzheimer's

Death came slowly
inching its way home,

Alzheimer's took him
long before
the end,
the old man died (as if he was alone)
his wife
unrecognised
as his best friend,

She cared for him
for close to twenty years
she wiped his arse
and fed him
with a spoon,

She made sure
that no one saw her tears

She learned that love
does not die
all that
soon,

He never knew how much
she had to give,
to make his last years
something he could bear,
she loved him
and she
made sure he could live

Such love, a hope
that everyone
should share,

They'd met,

a post war dance
on her dance card

She never thought that love could be
so hard.

Journeys

I was eighteen
when
I first read
"Songlines"
Bruce Chatwin
took me with him as he walked

from **dusty** plains...

...to long forgotten times,
and taught me
to see land
as if
it
talked,

The "Songlines"
is
the book I keep
with me,
a journey
of the spirit
and the mind,
where I first learned that

words

can set you free,
I read his life,
not knowing,
what I'd **find**,

His journey
came to end

as they all
must

a sorrow

never
spoken

and

unseen,
he left with words
unwritten
in
the
dust

but taught me

love

and gave me
writing's dream,

he died of aids
before it had
a name

his words
made sure
I'd never
be

the

same.

elementary my dear watson (crick your neck)

edna
lived a lonely half-life,
with cats and the loss of love,

he left her for a stripper,
wanted to explore
the stuff that's underneath the ordinary,

he'd say he loved her,
but always he was stringing her along,
the sort who thought it best

to let her down gently with lies,
a singing of those old blues tunes,
always life sings through the words,

and teaches us that we are just so small,
that we are just the lonely ones, the only ones,
forgetting light and dust that makes us whole,

that births us out of suns and strips us down to what we are,
children of this elemental world,
still, hidden.

Hometown

I'm home now, to hear the seagulls squawking
Over old chip bags, scavenging delights,
Fights and flights, you almost hear them talking,
Big fierce one-eyed bird wins bragging rights,

I'm home, to walk the streets that grew me up,
Three scruffy kids played footie in the park,
I went in goal and Brighton won the cup,
And no one cared we stayed out after dark,

I'm home to make a place for me to rest,
To hear the call and walk down to the beach,
Belong now to this town I love the best,
And once remembered dreams not out of reach,

I'm home for absence always has a cost,
To give my children that which I had lost.

These Days

"These are the burnt out ends of smokey days",
we are lilac-blind, cruel-blinded by our
give-up, press-reset, fifteen-minute ways,
this life through un-acquired tastes, seems sour,

These are the stubbed-out butts of dreams, of love,
each night we kiss our kids with whisky-breath
with our stale words and lies, it's not enough....
our bitter gift...a legacy of death,

These are, the cancer-ridden days of tears;
of drugs and dust and drought and forest fires,
in blind, cold pity we make real our fears,
look away with me as we light the pyres,

These are the fag-end days, the tipping point,
we're done, put out the light lock up the joint.

A poem for Lance on his birthday

What magic makes a poet, is it words?
A skill to weave them into something new?
Is it outlook, a sense of the absurd?
Innate gifts? possessed by very few?

Is it learning? acquired through many years?
With lonely nights spent reading lonely books?
Experience? acquired through many tears?
Or study of the world beyond its looks?

Perhaps it is a mix of all of this,
Perhaps to name it is to try too much,
Perhaps it is a thing we cannot list,
Or put in words, just know, but never touch.

For me? The heart, makes poets in the end
And Lance is one, true poet and true friend

The Jackson Poems

dusty time of night

dusty time of night
between dusk
and not sleeping
in your arms,

lonely walks the street
he's a blues song
looking for a home
rain-dirty love, all gone,

sunset slipped him a slow beer
steered him to a whisky-warm dive
bought him another round,
an empty bottle

is still full of memories.

fublin' with midnight

dirty street-light-nights, new cross
rain-tossed-laughter
a smokey pub
and last orders,

stumblin' home
in arm bound love
kissing in the rain
tastes clearer,

midnight fublin' trips us to the bed
instead of trying to move
just lie there, waiting for dawn
and for love, to never end.

1am ghost

i hear the late bars chucking out
drunken shouts and a police siren
i could not love this town more
if it were made of gold,

cat window scratches
i move slowly, not to wake her
a thankful purr to be rain-safe
and settles,

awake now
i set the sound to low
crackle-needle finds tom waits
in growling-soft saturday tones,

sit back and gently watch her,
breathe my hopes
like whisper-wishes
to the ghosts of night.

Sunday morning blues

the words won't come
on a sunday morning
never know what to say
the day after...

a bottle of jack
still sat on the table
accusing
the quiet morning,

she dresses quickly
says she has work
we kiss
friendly,

silence is my blues
it follows my heart
in dark shadows
and unsaid words.

dirty streets

crisp-packet, gutter-blows
under a grey london sky
and the left-overs
of rain,

new cross train station
on a sunday morning
is a noisy whore
all naked and unashamed,

the clack of the carriages
as they carry me town-bound
sooth my mood
un-silence my smile,

window gazing,
south london
all dirty in its beauty
all dirty, in its love.

love song in echo

i see the lovers
walking hand in hand
the unslept streets,

i see the lovers
kiss-touch-love
the undreamt years,

i see the lovers
echo-kissing
it aches my soul.

the tender blues

it's the gentle-soft
half-touches
that wear away
the first,

love is in the detail
not loud gestures
noisy flowers
and sex,

the tender blues
painted our silence
into ordinary days
quietly,

no one notices
where you are
or what song is playing,
until you get there.

last train home

tom waits
sings a jersey-girl lullabye
gravel-love
through tinny headphones,

train stops
ten minutes short of home
half hour delay
ain't that always the way,

smiles at raindrops
kiss-chasing
slowly
down dirty windows,

knows he is happy
just here, just now,
and that
is a quiet sadness.

a new coat of paint

dust covers
placed with love
over the scratched old gramophone
gently,

colour-faded walls
of the old home
need
touching,

a paint-peeled kiss
lingers in the room
unspoken
unheard,

the rain-tears
echo louder
in the empty room,
some things can't be fixed,

just painted
over.

The SoBo Sonnets

poetry

i met that old whore, poetry, she'd been
working out of "swallows", the brothel just
off the old steine, wrong side of thirty-five
and her good looks all needle-marked, and sharp

with the dead-drawn eyes of those who have been
fucked by sad old men and spotty kids, she
asked for a few quid, promised to publish
me in her next collection, the joke is

i don't give a shit, but slipped her a score
so long as she made it quick and didn't
spit. i remember her, from back in the
nineties, real looker, life took her the

hard way. some things are best left unspoken.
sometimes sonnets must just be left...broken.

one of us

i've never written through tears before, but,
he was and always will be, one of us,
one of this inter-connected uncut
world, a hero who never knew he was,

a hero for bringing such love into
this ugly world, into the lives of all
those who never even met him, or knew
his smile close up, he taught us not to fall

short in our humanity, in our love,
he reflected the best of this cruel world
through those around him, parents who could love
no more, friends touched with beauty, love unfurled,

he was and always will be, one of us,
a child i never knew, but full of love.

time-travel

talking to two german girls, and one is
dani, and without knowing, suddenly
its 1984, and i still miss
her, daniela sauter, so quietly

the memories surface, that coffee shop
in stuttgart, then the fernsehturm, and me
so scared of heights, but worth it, as i got
that kiss, and running through the rain, so free

of care, unaware that life is also
cruel; every heartbeat that we could not touch,
not feel, seemed eternal, but we must go
through such intensity to know how much

love is truly worth, when old enough to
feel its aching fire; always old, always new.

@ nite

the day ends, a burnt out smokey sunset,
the nite crawls under the door, a drunken
stranger you met in the pub and can't get
rid of, he sits in the corner, sunken

eyes give the lie to his feigned happiness,
tells you all his troubles, but every time
you think he is about to leave he tests
your patience with one more story, it's fine

you say, have some whiskey you say, there's beer
in the fridge if that is better, and soon
you find you are one with the nite, the fear
you felt takes a shot from each glass, the moon

outside sighs at the time you choose to lose,
you choose to be less than you are...you choose.

night swimming

i let the sea hold me, lie back and drift
in the setting-sun sky, all i can see
is elemental; solitude is gift
enough today, all i can feel is free,

is alive, i am becoming me once
more. i lie back and whisper a prayer to
the gods of sky and water; i know loss,
but here, now, i just feel alive, made new

out of broken pieces, scraps bound for
the seashore, driftwood-beautiful, i just
let the gentle tide kiss me to the shore
and i know who i am, and what i must

do and be, night-swimming gives me back my
life, shows me the wide blue horizon sky.

who am i?

i know, it's an old question, but a friend
asked me over dinner, i wasn't
sure what to say "a poet", in the end
was what i said, maybe, but it isn't

nearly the whole of me, a father, yes,
a husband, hardly; but who do i want
to be, i like to be alone, but guess
that does not define me, "loner", i can't

just leave it at that, there are many truths
that i am not brave enough to share, to
dare to reveal, and i have grown so used
to hiding that it is second nature to

me, but who am i? the truth is i am
learning, growing, and finding what i can.

days & nites

they blur, not the blur of speed, but that one
you get when watercolor paints slowly
drift into a sunday dawn. it is done
without me knowing, almost cagily

as if i am no longer living, but
being watched in a film, the character
who cannot see the obvious. it cuts
to the end, no happy ever after

just an endless question, what happens next...
and the answer echoes, a trick with smoke
and mirrors, it hides the lack of subtext,
it hides the life the character would choke

on if he saw it....nothing happens,
an endless horizon. nothing happens.

firestarter

i feel my fingers itching, i want to
build a bonfire of my poems, watch them
as they curl and blister, turning into
specks of ash to float away. once again

i have reached a point of emptiness, i
want to love what i have written, but do
not, most i can't even bare to read. my
theory is that any poet, any who

are good, will write at most five poems worth
the read, some days i think my five are done,
at other times that nothing on this earth,
will help me write five, nor even just one.

so i will be a firestarter, a
"twisted firestarter", for just today.

thoughts

"the wild catastrophe of mountains" is
a line from a poem i once read, can't
remember who or what, but the line twists
my mind. there are people like that, who aren't

just people, but mountains, and their souls take
us to new understanding, of love, pain,
of all the things in this strange life that make
us human. they are gifts that contain

the great song that echoes always through this
odd universe, they are people who teach
us how to see, people i would not miss
knowing for the world, their smiles alone reach

further than most love can dream of. henry
is such a mountain, locked, but inside free.

day-sleeper

i have become a day-sleeper, always
prone to insomnia, i now have just
given in. i snooze away these long days
and only get up when i really must.

it suits my mood, this darkness, let's me be.
while others dream of summer sunshine, i
am happy to be left alone, set free
from the chattering nonsense of blue sky

lovers, from the endless need to appear
happy. the night does not try to cheer me
up, accepts me as i am, has no fear
for me. the night does not have need to see

me settled or sorted, cured in some way
of illness that is me, so keep the day.

brighton 2am

for Sergio

brighton 2am, and again i am
walking home; sergio, a good friend from
italy is going home, we all can
learn from his love of life, his flame, not gone

pale in this dark world. tonino, as bright
a spark as you will ever meet somehow
steals clothes; he cycles through the naked night
and loves it, sergio, nude but not now

caring, drunk on happiness, and much beer;
but more than that, drunk on friendship, we all
love him as a brother, will keep him near
our hearts as he departs; we'll hear the call

of his longing to return, before he
even knows that he'll be back, just you see.

sunday 16th june 2013

sunday was sunshine, playing footie with
my kids down by the beach; and we talked, a
little, just the usual stuff, but some give
and take. none of the hurt will go away

but nor will the love. there is no choice for
me, things done cannot be undone, can
they be forgiven, each of us not sure,
i don't think i am the right kind of man

to forgive. she has bought tickets for paul
weller, end of june in london, all four
of us will go, and it will be like all
the bad days never were, and then before

i wake the dream will end, and i will know,
for us there's still such a long way to go.

ten minute sonnet

if i had ten minutes to live what would
i do, not write a sonnet that's for sure,
i'd want to be with loved ones if i could,
let them know how much i love them before

i went. i might quite like a cup of tea,
blackcurrant fruit tea, warm but not too hot,
with ginger nut biscuits, that would do me
nicely. as for things, what is there i've got

that i would miss? just friends and family.
you can keep all the material shit,
it won't matter to me, when finally
it's time for me to go, why would it.

so if i had ten minutes left to live
it is just love that i would want to give.

sunrise

i find the sunrise waiting for me, its
reds and golds held close to its face,
i can only tell you that brighton fits
my soul, and if there is the fainest trace

of other towns, and other times, i did
not leave them there on purpose. sunrise here
is far beyond my words, is joy i hid
from for so long, my empty, unnamed fear

of knowing i belong, of knowing i
must make my home among the driftwood and
the lonely, there is only the blue sky
to wait for us, to turn our dreams to sand

and laugh with the gulls. we must remember
who we are, where we're from, dawns dark ember.

thoughts (broken sonnet)

my thoughts are far away with friends i do
not know, poetry is cheap and pointless
on days like these. the world is both cruel and
beautiful. my thoughts are selfish, wanting

to be helpful to ease my pain, i am
not a good man by nature, but by the
cheap thrill it gives you to be dressed up as
good, "kleider machen leute", indeed they

do. my thoughts will not let go, of all the pain
i've seen, not mine, but parents who have loved
their children more than you would think possible,
and children, who have brought more love into

this world than most can see, but by being
who they are, they help us towards seeing.

poem after reading "this wonderful perpetual beautiful"

we are all poets, and none of us are,
none of us know what we are, none of us,
none of us are buddhists, but we all are,
we are all buddhist poets, all of us,

and none of us; buddhist poets should be
handled with care, avoid contact with eyes,
do not expose to naked flame, must be
washed separately, do not tumble dry,

buddhist poets must be switched off if near
medical equipment and must not be
tackled by the public, if seen stay clear,
if cornered can turn nasty, let them be;

we are all buddhist poets, all of us,
none of us know what we are, none of us.

carving love

there is a tradition in wales, to make
a carving out of wood, to make it for
your betrothed, to show you will not forsake
their love, that all those who have gone before

are made of little more than need, dressed up
as passion. for you, i have carved my heart
out of bloodwood, and even as my blood
flowed it loved you, you are forever part

of me, my chiseled fingers fumble to
hold you, fumble to make some beauty real
enough to speak of how i feel for you,
there is no part of me you cannot steal,

no part of me that is not yours, i see
the love/pain in your eyes, it sets me free.

letter to a friend (who is me)

we are all broken, that is the secret
we all hide from ourselves, however hard
we try to run from the pain of regret
we will never be free, we are all scarred

by it, but slowly, gently, if we love
and surround ourselves with those who love us,
then scars become little more than the stuff
of fading memories, so do not fuss

over regrets, there is only ever
now, and only ever this life, so look
to the sky spread your wings and fly, never
let others be your only self, it took

you close to the crow road, don't walk that way
again, remember, each one's a new day.

debris

sorting through old bags left at a hostel
i find the debris of hurried lives, so
much stuff left behind, a sadness as well
as some fun, odd things we leave when we go

without thought. a tube of anusol (with
applicator) many, many odd socks,
some swimming goggles, denim jeans well lived
in, two phone chargers, travel alarm clock,

several books i'd never want to read, mills
and boon, large print, some unused condoms, a
pocket gardening guide. all this just spills
out of bags and cases, left months, not days,

and saddest of all, a well-loved teddy
(he's safe, if they return he'll be ready)

some days are friends

some days are friends. this tuesday is one, they
don't know me, across this ether but i
know them, know little of the pain they may
be going through, but i hold them as high

as any people i know. they are the
best of us, unconditional love is
not in words but actions, we only see
it in the strength of real love. it lives

in a 3am scream of pain, when your
son cannot tell you, but you know; you are
closer to love then, than all those before
you. i love these odd friends though they are far

from my life, but sometimes you just know, you
hurt the truth of what they are going through.

poem after reading thomas kenney

4am, again, i'm out looking for
jesus on brighton's dirty streets, old jack
told me he'd seen him down the steine, he scored
some white before a fight broke out, out back

of the queens pub. my friend danny said he
saw him eyeing up the rent boys, top of
st. james street, sharing out fags like candy,
but you can't always trust your friends. some soft

lad called joe (you know, one piss short of the
bucket) said he sleeps next to him, every
night at the shelter, but i doubt joe sees
straight by that time, cheap wine and whiskey.

i keep walking, down to the brown mile, chat
to ghosts of friends i used to know; head back.

4am

these 4am brighton streets are my friends,
they hear my worn-out brogues make echoes in
the still night, they sip red wine for me, tend
to my weary thoughts, teach me to begin

again, to learn the beauty of the night,
to learn that i am loved by this nearly
dawn sky, this fickle sea, the thought i might
one day leave this town is said in barely

hushed tones, i left once, never again, i
know where i belong, where i am home, take
me down to the old steine, to where the sky
is brighton grey on a summer's day, make

me walk these dirty streets to find my love
against the gas works wall, that is enough.

bluesin' tuesday

sat listening to tom waits' gravel-slow
drawl, tuesday hits the window panes in rain-
drops and sadness, i watch the grey sky go
through its don't ask me why moods; there's no pain

worth a slow tear that doesn't begin in
the blues and end with a kiss, you know the
one, all butter-lips , makes your body sing
to the sway of sweaty hips and dirty

lovin'. there's no pain that can't be undone
by putting on a crackly old l.p.
letting the needle kiss you its dust-sung
tones, and low moans of a bluesin' whiskey-

coughed tuesday, sometimes that's all you need. light
me up from a pack of ten...it's our night!

language

more than twenty years ago a tutor
(who still wore elbow patches and denim)
told me that all language is metaphor,
i laughed at the idea, could not begin

to understand the concept, that words are
made of images, the first steps we took
on our long road to language were by far
the hardest, we saw the world, took one look

and said...i am, this is, we are; and then
began the great dreaming, the singing to
life of every creature, and once again
the songlines echo down the years, go through

from our beginning, in the word, to the
slow won knowledge, that language will just be.

a grey friday in may

friday is grey because i miss you. i
do not want you back, but i do want you.
i want to hold you, i want you to lie
to me, lie with me as we make it through

another day pretending everything
is ok. i cannot drown this ache, nor
sleep it off, i can't bear to wear this ring,
it digs into my bones; what is love for

if this is what it becomes, not hate, but
loss and emptiness, i never signed up
for this, i'd rather be stuck in our rut,
pretending to life, than have it all stop

and have to wake up, be brave enough to
look up at the sky, and make this world new.

thursday tears

sunshine woke me for a walk along my
seafront, went from hove down to the palace
pier, the gentle blue sea asking me why
i had not been there sooner, shown my face

to the morning sky. ambling back, there
is an old man, bench-sat, flat-capped, holding
a bunch of yellow roses, as he stares
tear-faced towards the ground, i am thinking

of walking by, but i just have to pause,
"are you ok?" he looks at me, simply
says, "this was where we met, '52 was
a sunny spring", i listen willingly

as he tells me of her, grief is not in
words, our thursday tears is where it begins.

desert

warm sirocco winds are your breath, sent fast
across the med to bring your dusty taste
to europe. my mind hears you, shadows cast
across my dreams, sahara, you don't waste

your words telling me your age, you saw
man take his first steps on africa's dry
savannah, you watched the stones, dragged for
the pyramids as your sands met the sky,

and you kept silent as the white man came
to rape and steal a continent, he took
your people to build america, shame
he never stopped to hear your song, to look

at your beauty. i hear you across the
years, as your sand drifts down towards the sea.

sunday sea

i walked down to the sunday sea, all green
and grey on a rainy brighton day, i
love its fierce temper and all the unseen
whispers of its waves aching to the sky,

this is my sea, not the fierce atlantic
nor the vast pacific, this gentle stretch
of water, the english channel; frantic
seagulls fight for food scraps along the beach,

soggy chips discarded in the rain, left
as day-trippers scurry, out of rain to
the noisy safety of the pier; the theft
of sunshine is no loss to me, i knew

days like this and grey sunday seas grew me
up long ago, became me, set me free.

imperfect

our imperfections complete us, they make
us real, they are who we are, and when we
learn to see that, to accept ourselves, take
us for what we really are, then we see

that we are all the same, that we are all
fragile and human, delicate beyond
belief. the flaws may be giants, or small
pale irritations, but if they were gone

we would be less than we are now, without
them we cannot grow, cannot learn to fly,
to breathe the wind, find highest mountains, shout
till our lungs are dry, leap and touch the sky,

how can a man who knows no fear learn to
conquer demons, to make himself anew.

moment

take this moment and kiss me with it, as
if it were the first time, and forever; take
this memory of love, make sure it has
the colours right, the touch, the scent, and make

it my eternity, to lift me when
i need. take this moment and cry with me,
with tears of loss brought back to me again
through thought, or word, or song; wipe eyes to see

that this too is real; to hold that time, that
grief inside of you, is to know that you
have loved, and will live again; don't look at
life as time, but as moment, and then through

those eyes know here and now is all we have,
and sharing moments from the past, is love.

flight

we cannot run from ourselves, our ghosts will
always follow us, we may as well try
to lose lonely shadows on a sun-still
day, however fast or far we may fly

memories drag us back to ourselves, back
through the times that made or broke us, they take
no pity on our weary hearts, they stack
up, card houses, fragile, ready to break,

tumbling razor blades cutting old wounds
till they bleed our very souls. we must learn
to be still, to hear the beauty, the sounds
of our lives that calm us, the silence earned

through sharing friendship and giving little
pieces of us, and so become less brittle.

elemental

i walk barefoot towards the beach, across
the grass of hove lawns, still muddy, still cold
in early spring, i feel the dewy moss
of dawn and let the fire of sunrise hold

my heart, renew my soul, across the steps
down to the shingle-chattery shore; for
me, the horizon, sea and sky have leapt
red-burned from the night-kissed dark. before

man took his first steps, spoke his first word, there
must have been such magic as this, such
elemental beauty sung through the air
and water of this world. i want to touch

that time, breath it in and keep it with me
as i trace steps, down to the lonely sea.

winter in april

it snowed again today, the icy wind
tasted sharp against my chapped lips and face,
it is as if we have committed sins
against nature herself, we're shown our place.

the sadness of these mad un-seasons meets
my mood perfectly, i am these cold grey
days, i am the cruel darkness that defeats
all hope. it is a part of me that may

not show in summer-moods and tender words
of love, but it is there, ever waiting
with blackest thoughts that will not go unheard,
and i know the grey days are beginning;

it snowed again today, and i became
winter in april, silent, dark, untamed.

departures

it is in the leaving that we learn love
has a cost, not the easy joy and thrill
of beginnings, but the hard pain, enough
to hurt us soul-deep, an aching loss, till

we can hardly bear it, wearing it hard
on our faces, a badge of honour. it
is in the leaving that we earn the scars
we bring to the next one we love, they fit

us as old clothes, comfortable in our
bitterness, only slowly allowing
them to be healed, by touch, and kiss, and hours
of talking, and it is in the sharing

that we grow, let go of old departures,
finding truth and beauty in new pictures.

time

time, does not exist, is just the whisper
of our need. we cannot comprehend the
simple truth, there is only now; transfer
your thoughts to the moment, let yourself be;

no more or less than that, just be. we try
so hard to plan our lives, we strive to make
them richer, put money aside to buy
happiness later, all we do is take

away the beauty in each day. the sun
still rises, the rain still bites, winter-sharp
on brighton streets, and when our lives are done
can we say we stood rain-joyful and laughed.

time does not exist, be careful not to
miss life, trying to make it better, new.

take these broken wings

for nina simone

"they call you little sorrow", how can they
see behind your eyes? they know so little
of the pain you pretend has flown away;
i see you, little bird, love so brittle

it breaks my heart to feel its echoes, to
taste the faint heartbeat of self, i would teach
you to fly, build you wings out of love, so
you can leap soul-strong towards the sky, reach

up and breathe the wind, glide on the gusts, the
beauty-silence that is solitude, let
me hold you with my words, so you can be
the genius you are, the one who gets

into our souls, with poet-songs that fly
on music, gifted from the lonely sky.

silence as friday

some days are silence, they are an unmade bed,
they begin in grey skies and dirty light,
they walk alone along the seafront, head
down to the beach just to stay out of sight

of conversations they no longer care
about. some days are emptiness, they sleep
alone, oblivious to all and stare
at empty walls, crying, they fight to keep

the tears from falling, loudly as they do.
some days are solitude, they keep their own
company, content just to make it through
to night, to sleep and let the dreams be sown

that bring lighter shades and warmer days, so
silence can be tucked tight away, let go.

21 grams of string theory

imagine our universe, as just one
neutron in another universe, it
must be so, infinity makes the sums
add up, or down, but how does that fit

with all we know of life? just look into
another's eyes for five minutes and see
the secrets of eternity, right through
the 21 grams they say our souls weigh;

we feel this connection, these vibrating
strings of matter, in music, art, and in
our own humanity, this understanding
is called god by some, i like to begin

with the word, and that word for me is love,
the truth is plain, that's what we are made of.

games

when you step back and watch, it's easy to
see the games we play, her hand touching his,
left there a moment too long, to see through
these subtleties is my game, i don't miss

the way people sit, angled next to each
other, the tip of her head, his laugh at
her poor joke, and when she moves she reaches
out to brush some dust off his coat, that

moment says she already owns him, she
has marked her territory, in return
he holds her gaze, allowing eyes to speak,
putting the moment on a low, slow burn,

the fun for me is watching those who do
not know that love is where they're heading to.

worn out

i have a pair of old boots, tackety
kick-about boots, laced with red string, and love.
i've had them more than thirty years, i see
no reason to change them now, though the scuff

marks cover the beaten up leather, like
the lines on my face. they are an old friend,
comfortable at my worst; they have hiked
me round europe, thumbs out; and in the end

they have lasted longer than most of the
people I thought important in my youth.
they have seen me drunk, and sat quietly
in the corner as i made love. the truth

is they are part of me, worn out
or not, they are mine forever; no doubt.

a day

if you had to choose one day, one perfect
day, what would it be? that drop goal, you know
the one, wilkinson! does beauty effect
you, the bedruthan steps with a rainbow

kissing the sea and sand, lifting your heart?
or perhaps the birth of your child, who can
not be in love with that day, to feel part
of something so magical, that it stands

alone in our hearts. for me, it's easy,
sunday 9th of june 1991,
sometime after 10pm, suddenly
i knew what love was, it lived in that one

kiss, in that one moment, i can still taste
it, and know that love is never wasted.

iridescence

a dusty, scuffy love has coloured my
life, and in it you have been my iris,
my rainbow in an iridescent sky,
i see you differently each day, my wish

is to know each side of you, to see your
smile from every angle, to see inside
your soul, to know what dreams were yours before
i met you, and give them back to you, tied

with my heart. your beauty shimmers through the
flesh of me, aching into my bones, and
time is silent, it sleeps through the days we
are together, and leads us by the hand

to that one moment, when we make sense,
two souls as one, becoming iridescence.

the beauty-beast

if i had the skill i'd carve a jaguar,
a beauty-beast to hold our dreams, its eyes
would burn bright through amazon nights, grown hard
and bitter-fierce with forest fires, its eyes

would hold me, all of my beauty, all of
my ugliness, love-hate that tears us, its
eyes would be the very tears of love,
the tears that speak to us of all the bits

of life we dismiss as pointless dreams, that
we choose not to see. if i had the skill
i'd make a beauty beast to show us what
we are, scarred by our greed, without the will

to change, a beauty-beast with eyes of fire
reflecting back to us our dark desires.

end of time

winter surprised us, early march brought snow
instead of bluebells. we feel it in the
seasons, each year stranger than the last, so
we turn up the heating, and dare the sea

to rise. on the news today they told us
that in ten years antibiotics will
no longer work and all the careful trust
we put in medicine, and all the skill

of science will not stop it. we will die
from cut fingers and childbirth, from all
the patient bacteria, that will try
to cull our busy species, this is small

compared to the next great fall, when the earth
(called gaia) shows us what we're really worth.

"to define something is to give it limits"

words capture us, they hold us in their thrall,
they steal our dreams and make us less than we
can be, we do not know ourselves at all
when we allow their subtle chains to be

the meaning of our lives. they sit in wait
and mug us when we are not looking, "son",
"brother", "husband", "father", i was too late
in seeing that i am just me, long gone

are the days when i tried to be what i
am not, when i tried to live the words that
defined me, now i am free, as the sky
is free, i look up, unafraid of what

i am called, unafraid to be alive,
let words be what they are, i will survive.

rain as colours for my soul

the rain blows off the channel and into
all the mortar cracks, old buildings, weary
as this town can be, shrug, then shiver through
the late winter chill. i walk along the

seafront, hood down, letting the rain hit hard
against my face, it means i am alive
if i can feel the sting of it, some shard
of being, some pulse within in me still strives

for feeling, to let these tears mingle with
the rain and disappear. i love this town
in winter, all buttoned up, aching, stiff
after the summer madness, i walk down

to the beach, throw stones into the sea and
feel my soul lift, as rain joins sky and land.

not quite a love poem (written on the back of a tesco's receipt)

i love you like cottage cheese, squeeze you all
over me. i love you like those salad
bowls they sell down isle one, cruchy small
ones, not the limp curly ones i once had

by mistake. my love for you is cheap, like the
basics garlic bread, 32p but
very tasty if cooked just right, trust me
on that one. my love for you is hand-cut

cooked ham from the deli-counter, you have
to have some treats in life, to keep the spice
going. my love for you is money saved
on two for one offers, basmati rice

and balsamic vinegar, and all this
makes a meal that's truly worth a kiss!

black & white

you can only play jazz records in black
and white. it's the law. i met her in a
dodgy student bar, nottingham; way back
before the internet turned our world grey,

before we were trained to click "like"; monkeys
at a tea party. i met her, but did
not use the usual corny chat up sleaze,
stole her eyes and held her gaze, kept a lid

on my urge to speak, walked across no word
said, and just kissed her, passionate as if
we were long time lovers, no slap came, heard
her friends gasp. she kissed me back, her soft lips

thrilling my body. we had that one night,
did i steal her dreams? is it black and white?

black & white (ii)

i wish i could turn all your pain into
starlings, to fly south in this cold winter,
gathering on the old west pier, and through
the beatings of their wings let you gather

yourself again, be who you are, be where
you want to be. i have seen love many
times, and yours is real, a true loves dares
to be what it is, heeds no words from any

doubters. you have lived in the sun, i wish
i could let you know you are living there
still, that love knows no distance, and to kiss
"the one" is every dream come true. i care

about you in this odd place, but more than
that, we are friends, and i'll do what i can.

black & white (iii)

our love was a sadness of starlings, the
old west pier flew them south and made winter
of us. home now for ten years, how could we
not see how our love became so bitter,

our first date, twenty years asleep now, was
all i ever wanted, casablanca
at the roxy in brixton, and because
you were late, i nearly ran; to lose the

thrill of kissing you that night, would be to
cut my arm off. i wanted to be your
bogart and you bacall, to kiss you through
some black & white filter, was all the more

special, was the moment I wanted from
life, and i can't regret it now it's gone.

names

can i name the wind, can i tame it with
a word and make it sing for me, can i
use its power to lift me up and give
me joy, soaring, dreaming in the blue sky.

can i walk the songlines, breathing life to
the world with words so gently sung, naming
each bush, each creature, singing lonely through
the dreamtime, through the very taming

of the world. can i name you my love, catch
you in one word and make you mine, kiss your
tender lips as i speak it, make you match
it with your own, a word i'd not before

heard. names have power beyond believing
and words are magic beyond their meaning.

tastes of sunlight

dawn, an osmosis of light across charles
bridge. prague wakes our tired sheets, eases us
to life with the sounds of coffee, unfurls
our love-entwined body, we feel the loss

of night's fired beauty, but joy in the taste
of sunlight on our naked skin. the day
moves on, the city soft music, hastens
into a symphony, footsteps make way

for car horns as the tempo rises, and
we find ourselves with figaro at the
prague state opera, such a daunting, grand
and stunning building, we can almost see

the music, taste it as it echoes this
city of our hearts, that night, one last kiss.

cariad am byth (love forever)

it was old, it was old before the stars
and dust conjoined to make us, it is in
the very atoms of our souls and far
across the cosmos it echoes, begins

to sing of a welsh love, of homeland and
of loss. love is beyond time, it does not
die with the dying, it is not as sand
hourglass-slipping, but lasts, as the rocks

of st. brides bay stand wind-proud against the
fierce atlantic. it is marked on gravestones
and sings its beauty in the memories
of our hearts. bred in our very bones

and fires our blood. none who have loved
can doubt that it will always be enough.

like trying to juggle sand

like a cold wind on a sunny day, your
love blows me leaf-spun and bewildered, like
a salmon struggling upstream what more
is there for me but love and death, each might

give solace. like trying to speak a moment
in a word, you are my beautiful, as
you are my despair, we were not meant
to hurt each other, if love really was

supposed to be like this, then it would have
died a painful death in the lightning strike
of lust, and trying to give you what you crave
is like throwing teardrops at the sea. like

trying to catch butterflies in your hand
your love is like trying to juggle sand

age

age shook me awake at 2am, made me
get up and take a piss, laughed at me as
i stumbled downstairs, poured some jackie d
and lit me a cigarette. age put some jazz

record on the old player, crackled joy
bluesin' through the night, age told me to go
out and find some cheap floozy to enjoy
my bed with. age has always been there, so

many nights misspent and forgotten, give
way to a grey-whiskered face, no trace
of that young man who just wanted to live
for the moment under the devil's grace,

and die a blazing death to light up any
sky, now the reasons to live, are many.

silence

sometimes i need silence, i need it like
a hot bath, just lying there listening
to the nothing that is beauty. i might
spend an easy hour soaking, pretending

that i am far away from all the thoughts
that fly through my head, that will not let me
be, i close my eyes and let all my doubts
drift away like morning dew, gone slowly

with the rising sun. sometimes i just need
to be alone, to find that solitude
that gives me peace, let go the dreams that lead
to pain and madness. learn the fortitude

that comes with age, the truth so simple to
grasp, humanity is where love comes through.

love

today i am seventeen, swimming in
the pools of the tarn valley, i can
look in the mirror, not see the drawn skin
and grey whiskers, i can be myself, stand

alone in the cold night, and know that i
am loved, know that i have a friend who does
magic, a box of tricks flown from the sky
straight into my heart, friendship knows that love

is not in the gifts, but in the giving
that sometimes our pale words are not enough,
that love is a trust, a precious living
thing, that once found lasts through all the black, tough

days of despair and grows as a flower,
a beauty, a truth, the greatest power.

age as song

how is it this random collection of
atoms knows that it grows old, and weary
of the heady songs of youth, now my love
is a fading, crackling jazz song. we

no longer yearn to dance to faster
beats, those giddy, dizzy, wind-spun days are
tucked away in an old draw, and laughter
now eases its tired feet into a pair

of comfy slippers. i am happy my
life is now sung to ella's sweet tones;
to paul robeson's deep voice that meets the sky
and lifts the heart, touching my very bones

with its aching drawl. this is my song and
i sing with age, to show i understand.

city lullaby

city night, eases me to sleep with its
gentle song, traffic down on new church street
buzzes in the distance like insects, bits
of sunday morning 1am come sneak-

ing through the open window, the smell of
petrol fumes tingles across the room and
scratches like an old flea-bitten dog, cough-
ing i get up to close the window, stand-

ing for a moment just to listen to
my city; i hear the sirens down on
western road, the friday-night-kids go through
their peacock dance, but the drunks are too far gone

to care, and stare dumbly as the cops try
to move them on. my city, lullaby.

the only god i know is love

the only god i know is love, not the
soft-hard fire-fierce passion of people, nor
sex, though that is fine, put simply, for me
it is my love of humanity, born

out of a deep faith in my fellow man,
and sustaining me, holding me close through
the dark night we call life, with it i can
cope with all life has, highs and lows, stay true

to myself and love my friends, family
and those strangers, who brush against my world,
passing briefly by, almost completely
unnoticed, but who help my soul unfurl

and grow into what it should be, a strong
love-voice for the weak, lonely, lost and gone

Ordinary Words

Poetry, for me, should let the reader
in, like an old friend, come round for coffee,
talking together sharing, small, tender
moments, a love-touch. Poetry for me

should have layers, a deep pool to dive breath-
burning into, then surface-break, gasping
child-like joy at returning from the depths
of thought and tears, a razor's edge rasping

across your mind and heart. Poetry for
me should have a beauty in its sound, time-
less songs, bone-bred and sung soul-deep, restore-
ing spirits, allowing meaning slowly to unwind

towards a better understanding of
moment, thoughts, each other...and of love.

My thanks to Dale Winslow for her belief in my writing, her incredible patience as an editor and her friendship for which I don't have the proper words to repay her.

I am also very grateful to Ian Marshall for the wonderful photograph and to Stephen Roxborough for using it to design the cover.

A big thank you must go out to everyone who has read my work and given me feedback. There are far too many to mention, and you all know who you are, but to single out a few thanks to Debs, Larry, Lance, Chris, Fiona, Rich, Stefan, Erin, Chuck, Doc, Rose, Tarringo, Don, Kami and Amanda, also a special thanks to Lowri whose conversations led to many of the SoBo sonnets. There are many reasons that have contributed to this book being produced and the online poetry community is a big one of those.

My gratitude also to the editors of all the journals, collections, magazines and ezines that have published me over the years. These include Poetry Monthly (UK), The Recusant, The Beat, ETC, Lit Up Magazine, The Copeland Love Poems Collection and most recently Rebel Poetry.

Thanks to my family. Their constant love through some difficult times has kept me going.

And lastly thanks to Anita, Alice and Josh for never letting me take all this too seriously, this book would not exist without you and I love you dearly.

Acknowledgements

Many of these poems have been published in various journals, collections, and e-zines including The Copeland Love Poems Collection, Poetry Monthly, Outside Writers, Carcinogenic Poetry, Eviscerator Heaven, Gloom Cupboard, The Recusant, InkSweat & Tears, The Plebian Rag, Heroin Love Songs, The BEAT, Cherry Picked Hands, blacklisted magazine, Heavy Bear, & lines written w/a razor.

About the Author

Si Philbrook spent twenty years working in the care sector for people with autism. He has also been a chef, a night porter, call centre worker and petrol station attendant. He lives in Brighton, UK. His poetry has been published in collections, journals, ezines and magazines in the US, Canada, Australia, Ireland and the UK. He was shortlisted for the 2010 Erbacce Poetry Prize. This is his first collection.

NeoPoiesis: *a new way of making*

1) in ancient Greece, poiesis referred to the
process of making: creation - production -
organization - formation - causation

2) a process that can be physical and
spiritual, biological and intellectual,
artistic and technological, material and
teleological, efficient and formal

3) a means of modifying the environment
and a method of organizing the self,
the making of art and music and poetry,
the fashioning of memory and history and
philosophy, the construction of perception
and expression and reality

4) an independent publisher with a steadfast
goal to print and promote outstanding
poets, writers and artists that reflect
the creative drive and spirit of the new
electronic landscape

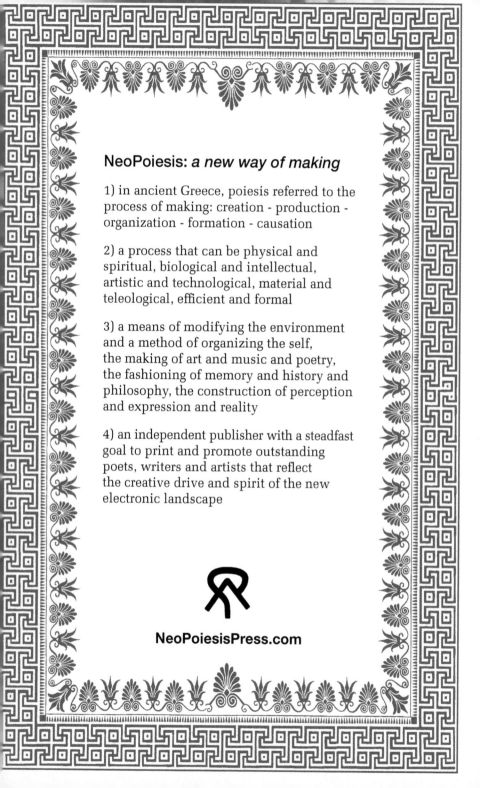

NeoPoiesisPress.com